282

WITHDRAWN

Aspects of
CHRISTIAN SOCIAL ETHICS

Aspects of

CHRISTIAN
SOCIAL ETHICS

CARL F. H. HENRY

Editor, *Christianity Today*

WILLIAM B. EERDMANS PUBLISHING COMPANY
GRAND RAPIDS, MICHIGAN

23296

TO ALL
WHO SHARE A PASSION
FOR APPLYING GOD'S TRUTH
TO THESE DISJOINTED TIMES

CONTENTS

INTRODUCTION

THESE ESSAYS, SOMEWHAT EXPANDED, COMPRISE THE 1963 PAY-
ton Lectures given at Fuller Theological Seminary under
the general subject "Aspects of Christian Social Ethics."
They do not provide a comprehensive exposition of Christian social theory, but they do discuss some of the contemporary issues in social ethics, and provide certain evangelical guidelines in strategic areas of Christian concern.

The twentieth century has cherished high hopes for socio-
politico-economic resconstruction. First it trusted mass education to propound a new vision of society, then domestic
legislation and possibly even international jurisprudence, and
more recently it has looked to mob pressures and revolutionary
techniques to bring about rapid social fulfillment. In the
performance of its mission in the world, even the Christian
Church was drawn to neglect its supernatural resources
and — in an apostate mood — relied instead upon education,
legislation and compulsive techniques to achieve social transformation. The disappointment that has followed hard on
these experiments should sober and sharpen our awareness
of man's hungers and needs. Much of the world is ready
now to respond to a message that offers fresh hope for
mankind, even if it emerges in the context of faith in the
living power of God, even if it fosters afresh a high sense of
personal duty. For its validity and vitality social theory requires both scriptural standards and moral power. Both
these requirements are violated when the expectation of

9

social change exceeds what certain fundamental forces are actually qualified to promise and to deliver.

The Church's primary duty is to expound the revealed Gospel and the divine principles of social duty, and to constrain individual Christians to fulfill their evangelistic and civic responsibilities. The Church certainly does have a vital stake in legislation; involvement in the social arena it neglects both to its own detriment and to the detriment of society. In an hour of widespread revolution, when political forces are reshaping the larger frontiers of modern life, the Church's concern with the problem of social justice is especially imperative. But how this social involvement is properly carried out — whether by the institutional Church acting in a political way, or by individual Christians conscientiously fulfilling their civic duties — is a very important question.

The prime need of the Church in these times is a new sense of its proper task. I cannot escape the conviction that, immense as the Christian stake in legislation and education and culture may be, the Church is grievously wrong to plunge into these concerns at the expense of neglecting its prior responsibilities toward the family and vocational calling. In Deuteronomy 6 the Shema charges the believer to guard the entrustment of his spiritual heritage to the next generation: "Now these are the commandments, the statutes and the judgments, which the Lord your God commanded to teach you . . . that thou mightest fear the Lord thy God, to keep all his statutes and his commandments, which I command thee, thou, and thy son, and thy son's son, all the days of thy life; . . . And these words, which I command this day, shall be in thine heart; and thou shalt teach them diligently unto thy children, and shalt talk of them when thou sittest in thine house, and when thou walkest by the way, and when thou liest down, and when thou risest up . . . . And when thy son asketh thee in time to come,

What mean the testimonies, and the statutes, and the judgments, . . . then shalt thou say unto thy son, We were Pharaoh's bondmen . . . and the Lord brought us out . . . . And the Lord commanded us to do all these statutes, to fear the Lord our God, for our good always, that he might preserve us alive, as it is at this day. And it shall be our righteousness, if we observe to do all these commandments before the Lord our God, as he hath commanded us." This passage reminds us also that the home is the best environment for teaching respect for law, as rooted ultimately in the divine order of things, and for creating a climate that lifts personal reverence for law above external compulsion. One child lost to the faith usually becomes a family lost to the faith, and not many generations later a whole community of unbelief is set in motion because of some earlier neglect of parental duties. A social concern that neglects the spiritual needs of those who stand in closest relationship to the moral agent can hardly hope to remedy the ailings of the human family in general.

The same problem concerns vocational calling. It would be impossible to estimate the spiritual blessings implicit in the universal consecration of work to the Lord. At the same time the failure of the Church in many instances to comprehend work as a spiritual service easily encourages its members to vocational delinquency and perhaps even to engagement in delinquent vocations. It is true, of course, that Christian influences in the home serve to shelter most young people from immoral vocations. But the fact remains that any work pursued without a sense of calling will lack spiritual vitality; instead, such a lack readily invites declension in the spirit of the worker, and in the quality and nature of his work. For the Christian Church to think of social action mainly in terms of political influence while discounting or ignoring its influence upon children and the world of work is sheer folly.

11

INTRODUCTION

Since state absolutism and its spirit of titanic government now seem rampant on every continent, it is imperative to stress what the New Testament insists upon, namely, that the Church has its own essential life. It is no mere adjunct of the State, nor do its authority and existence flow from the State. From the New Testament it is equally clear that the State also has its own essential life and an authority not derived from the Church. The New Testament does not, however, supply a definitive statement of how the separate entities of Church and State are to be ideally related. Because its authority comes from God, the State has an authority even over the believer (Romans 13); but for this very reason also, the believer will resist any State requirement that he disobey what God commands (Acts 5).

While the American experiment of Church-State separation has avoided the European error of establishment, it is now battling pressures that would compromise this principle in the direction either of "multiple" establishment (that is, Church-State partnerships in the achievement of sectarian goals) or of secularism (whereby the State, in its public institutions and affirmations, acts as if there were no God). Although the sad predicament of churches in totalitarian countries or in nations gripped by a state church should be plain enough, forces are continually at work to extend one or the other pattern to the American scene.

Most of the material in this volume was prepared in written form especially for the Payton Lectures, but the first two essays have been used previously over a period of time. The invitation as Payton lecturer, however, encouraged my organization of these essays in their present form. My years at Fuller Seminary as head of the Department of Systematic Theology (1947-1957) are a decade of treasured associations; the invitation by former colleagues to present the Payton Lectures therefore supplied a happy opportunity to share new convictions and to renew personal fellowship.

12

The opening essay, "Christianity and Social Transformation," was presented to the clergy of Berlin (American military chaplains also attended) during Evangelist Billy Graham's 1960 crusade in Germany. Since I refuse to identify Christianity as "a revolutionary religion" — as do many modern churchmen — a further comment on this theme seems appropriate, and it appears, accordingly, in the appendix under "Christianity and Revolution." "The Christian View of Work" has been given more widely — first as one of the (unpublished) Weber Memorial Lectures at Moravian Seminary in 1960, then at Gordon College commencement exercises, at Bethel College during Convocation and in Westmont College chapel. In 1959 I shared the material in Burma with 1200 Christian workers attending a World Vision pastors' conference. But this essay's most memorable use, perhaps, came in Essen, Germany, during the aforementioned Graham campaign. Carrying these convictions to the Rhineland, where pietistic Protestant parents reared Karl Marx, was an unusual opportunity indeed. A comprehensive exposition of work would need to present not only its religious role, but also its right, responsibility and risks — themes which I must postpone for some larger analysis of the subject.

The central essay on "The Christian Stake in Legislation" reflects convictions crystalized during my editorship of *Christianity Today*. This position has frequently brought me together with churchmen of different persuasions; sometimes we have met in highly volatile situations, then again in calm table talk concerning the Church's place in social action. The major principles of this subject I have registered in many discussions, including several national telecasts, in numerous off-the-record ecclesiastical consultations, and in material for *Christianity Today*. I owe some mention of appreciation to Senator A. Willis Robertson (Dem.-Viriginia) and Congressman John Anderson (Rep.-Illinois) for helpful suggestions on this chapter, and to Professor Gordon H. Clark of Butler University for comment on the whole.

The last essay, "The Nature of God and Social Ideals," stresses the importance of the evangelical emphasis on the equal ultimacy of God's justice and love, and traces aberrations of liberal and neo-orthodox social theory and method to the theological compromise of this biblical doctrine of God's attributes. In some respects, then, this closing essay is of fundamental import for the structure of social ethics.

I wish to thank my talented and devoted wife, Helga Bender Henry, for assistance without which the lectures could not have been readied for prompt publication, and my efficient secretary, Irma Peterson, for typing the manuscript.

— CARL F. H. HENRY

Christianity Today
Washington, D. C.

I. CHRISTIANITY AND SOCIAL TRANSFORMATION

THE CHRISTIAN TASK FORCE IS DIVIDED TODAY ABOUT THE best method for improving social conditions. The problem may be stated this way: In seeking a better social order, to what extent shall we rely on *law* and to what extent on *grace*? How much shall we trust *legislation* and how much shall we trust *regeneration* to change the social setting? What should we expect the *State* to contribute, what should we expect the *Church* to contribute, if we are seeking a society ruled by justice and love?

Many issues on which twentieth-century churchmen disagree, and laymen as well, turn on this question. It underlies the behind-the-scenes controversy between Billy Graham and Reinhold Niebuhr: whether the evangelist by his emphasis on spiritual decision and dedication offers a solution too simple for presumably insoluble social problems, and whether the professor by his reliance on legislation and compulsion as the means of social betterment minimizes and neglects the transforming power of the Holy Spirit. It is involved in one's attitude (if he takes a reasoned attitude) toward the crusade for civil rights and for racial integration. It is involved in the debate over government and public welfare: is the welfare state a normal exercise of governmental function (as the socialists would have it), or should the State (except in times of emergency) refrain altogether from welfare programs?

In our century, as I see it, Protestant forces seeking a

better social order in America have mostly neglected the method of *evangelism* and the dynamic of supernatural *regeneration* and *sanctification*. Instead, they have resorted to a series of alternative forces — at first, moral propaganda and education, then legislation, and more recently, non-violent public demonstrations and even mob pressures against existing laws. Now it is true that the Church has a legitimate and necessary stake in education and legislation as means of *preserving* what is worth preserving in the present social order, but it must rely on spiritual regeneration for the *transformation* of society. The neglect of this latter resource accounts mainly for the social impotence of contemporary Christianity.

Social action begins, of course, only where there is some sense of the immorality of the *status quo,* a witness against social evils, and a creative challenge to the established attitudes and patterns of society. Social passivity is no strategy at all. Hence we ignore that mood of indifference settling on some churches in their recoil from Protestant liberalism's substitution of social betterment for spiritual redemption. In these churches the sole preoccupation is private saintliness, preaching "Christ crucified" in absolute isolation from socio-political affairs, and promoting the piety of the local church in total unconcern over social disorders and evils.

The reconstruction or renewal of society may be attempted through a number of different strategies. In this essay we will compare, contrast, and evaluate some of the strategies used by agencies in this fast-fading twentieth century, hoping thereby to gain a greater insight into the best social strategy for the Church.

1. CONTRASTING SOCIAL STRATEGIES

Speaking broadly, the major methods proposed for social change today may be identified as the strategies of *revolution, reform, revaluation,* and *regeneration.* Before characterizing these methodologies in detail, a preliminary definition will serve to distinguish them. All four terms, indeed, share the Latin prefix *re*, but this prefix bears a variety of meanings and signifies either repetition, restoration, or reversal (of a former act, position, or state).

By *revolution* we mean the radical change of social patterns, in their essential constitution, through violence and compulsion. By *reformation* we mean that gradual but pervasive ethical amendment of particular abuses which secures a decisive improvement of prevailing social character and forms. By *revaluation* we mean a fresh intellectual comprehension and direction, whereby social life and structures are critically reassessed in the light of transcendent moral norms. By *regeneration* we mean transformation by supernatural impulse in individual lives whereby the social scene is renewed through a divine spiritual motivation.

These terms may seem in some respects to have somewhat arbitrarily assigned meanings. But we shall proceed to examine the four strategies at closer range in order to establish the propriety of these definitions.

The strategy of *revolution* not only proposes to rectify social evils, but it denies the existence of divinely given structures in history and society. It would destroy and displace *ultimate norms*, whether in respect to marriage, property, or the State. The obvious example in modern times is Communism. In place of the time-honored social forms validated by revealed religion, and still widely accepted as normative by society in general, Communism substitutes novel patterns of social life based on the totalitarian state, which takes control of family, of economic and political life, and of culture itself. Communist theory assails the *status quo* along lines that are anti-Christ (that is, it opposes Christian patterns of marriage, economics, and limited government) and anti-God (since it opposes the whole idea of supernaturally willed orders of responsibility).

17

The strategy of *regeneration*, by contrast, expresses the classic Christian view. It deplores any socio-historical revolt against the divine order of creation, while through spiritual renewal it seeks to secure man's respect for, and return to, the divine intention in society. The purpose of redemption, therefore, is to bind man's will afresh to the purpose of the Creator and the Lord of life.[1]

Both the strategies of *revolution* and *regeneration* express indignation over the *status quo*; the one is fundamentally destructive of the past and the other reconstructive of it; the one radically anti-supernaturalistic and the other radically anti-naturalistic. The former brings the whole socio-historic movement under the criticism of Marx in order to destroy it, and the latter under the criticism of Christ in order to renew it.

Between these opposite poles we may locate the strategies of social *reform* and of social *revaluation*. While both aim to revise the existing social situation, neither involves a critique as radical as that of *revolution* or of *regeneration*. Why do *reform* and *revaluation* lack thoroughgoing indignation over the cultural order? The *reform* strategy builds upon the developmental (that is, evolutionary) philosophy of a gradually emerging ideal society.[2] The *re-*

[1] One can sympathize with, and yet disown, the growing tendency to describe Christianity as a "revolutionary" religion. In favor of this idea one may range all the elements that establish the uniqueness of biblical religion, from special revelation to special incarnation and special redemption. Something may be said, too, for calling all competitive views "reactionary" because none of them holds the potentiality for supernatural transformation. But revolution is the overthrow of the old by the new, whereas biblical religion is essentially restorative rather than destructive; the work of redemption looks back to the work of creation. Moreover, churchmen who speak of Christianity as revolutionary are too often found supporting modern reactionary and revolutionary ideals in the name of Christ. (See the extended note on "Christianity and Revolution" in the appendix.)

[2] The concept of "reform" long had a sounder evangelical sense in and through the Protestant Reformation and "Reformed" thought. But

valuation strategy, on the other hand, emphasizes transcendent values discoverable in human experience. Both approaches, therefore, must find in the presently existing social order a significant area of contact. They have this difference, however: since the *reform* strategy must always consider the present as a necessary plateau to the next emerging level, it therefore lacks a deeply indignant criticism, and also any fixed criterion of judgment. Appeal to the process of evolution in the interest of social change (and presumably progress) necessarily rules out durable meaning and worth; it substitutes transient for transcendent social principles. Since the *revaluation* strategy appeals in its critique of culture and society to permanent values, it escapes these difficulties in principle. But this reliance on transcendent criteria, in turn, experiences constant jeopardy, not only through its association with evolutionary theory, but especially through its failure to exhibit a cosmic justification (as revealed theology does) for unchanging norms and values.

2. CONTRASTING ROLE OF THEOLOGICAL REALITIES

From an evangelical perspective the essential difference between these strategies is apparent in three ways: (1) the connection they maintain or disclaim between social action and theological priorities; (2) the dynamisms by which they propose to revise the social order; and (3) their attitudes toward the Church in relation to social change. In the present section we will discuss the first of these.

The historic Christian view sets the social problem in the larger theological framework of divine revelation and redemption, and cultural objectives in the context of the Chris-

---

social reform as such is today largely a humanistic concern, seeking to advance new structures and not to redeem a fallen order, and lacking biblical presuppositions and supernatural orientation. For that reason it seems preferable to speak of the Christian view in terms of the strategy of regeneration.

tian mission. This fact distinguishes the strategy of *regeneration* from the other patterns of social action, in which the social issue tends to become ultimate. Christian leaders do not regard themselves primarily as social reformers. They give no quarter to the illusion that Christianity is primarily an ethical idealism engaged in denouncing political and social injustice, or aiming at social reform as an end in itself. Even in the social thrust they preserve Christianity's basic nature as a religion of supernatural redemption for sinners.

The radical rejection of a theological basis for social action is notably characteristic of Communism. The strategy of *revolution* must destroy every rival to the totalitarian state as the ultimate source and sanction of human rights and duties. Not only its dogmatic naturalism, but its special insistence on economic determinism as the fixed axis of historical process requires the unqualified rejection of whatever metaphysical principle might threaten this absolute. Here the affirmation of God (the supernatural in precise form) is repudiated as illusion, and as harmful illusion at that ("religion is the opiate of the people").

The strategy of *reform*, while often vigorously opposed to supernaturalism (and therefore to theology) as an explanatory principle, is usually less gladiatorial in its attitude toward religion (regarding it as a beneficent development in man's evolution). Humanism is a relevant example. But *reform* strategy considers speculative philosophy a more trustworthy avenue of knowledge than theology and tends to find the essence of religious experience simply in loyalty to ethical ideals and social values.

The *revaluation* strategy, by its emphasis on the priority of ideas and ideals, requires a spiritual interpretation of the cosmos which subordinates physical things to the ultimate categories of mind and value. With this commitment to transcendent norms, therefore, the next step is usually (as in most philosophies of idealism and the theistic religions) to an infinite self-conscious will, to a deity of a sort, in relation to which the social order finds its meaning and direction. The *revaluation* strategy, moreover, stresses the immanence of these ideals and values in human experience, or their universal accessibility to the minds of men. Thus it prizes every religion and philosophy compatible with this quest for ideals. It does not hesitate to find in Jesus Christ the highest example of human achievement of the ethical ideal, although it swiftly attaches this moral realization to its own schemes of metaphysics, and with bold originality spells out its supposed implications for modern social philosophy. But because it stresses the universal and immanent accessibility of truth and morality, the *revaluation* approach necessarily plays down the biblical teaching that all men are corrupted by sin and need a special supernatural rescue. *Revaluation* has more the character of an ideology than of a religion; in actuality it esteems philosophy of religion above theology.

The *regeneration* strategy insists that revelational theology is prior, and depicts the Living God as dealing simultaneously with man's spiritual and material condition. The Church derives her social message from divinely revealed principles. By contrast, the other strategies exalt the social issue above the theological, and prize the Christian religion mainly as a tool for justifying an independently determined course of social action. They show little concern for the Creator-Redeemer God and his holy commandments; for Palestine as the geographic theater of the drama of human destiny; for the specially-inspired Scriptures; for the Law and the Gospel; for the social crisis viewed within man's larger problem of created dignity and sinful corruption; and for human rights and responsibilities "under God."

In defining and delineating the fundamental perspectives of an ideal social order, the other strategies invoke moral criteria independent of the Bible. They do not all, like

Communism, rail at the commandments and scorn the Bible, although even humanists like Harry Elmer Barnes did not hesitate to deplore the ethics of Jesus. While they may prize the Bible for high moral insights, they nonetheless single out only those premises in the scriptural revelation congenial to their own presuppositions. Humanists treasure such generalities as democracy, brotherhood and justice, or other social conclusions presumably "inhering in the Christian Gospel" (in which they have no genuine interest whatever). Idealists hail Christianity as the supreme religion of ethical idealism whose primary end is social reconstruction. But capitalizing on the social and minimizing the personal message of Christianity, and thereby obscuring the special framework of revelation and redemption on which both depend, has serious consequences. By divorcing the social from the personal, it deals with human rights in abstraction from human responsibilities, or rather, from the divine obligation of man. It obscures the supernatural source and sanction of human rights and duties, and fractures them (Roosevelt's famous "four freedoms," for example) through loss of a comprehensive overview. Vagueness results just where precision is most needed today, that is, in stipulating the content of the life of social righteousness and personal virtue. It should surprise nobody, then, that in respect to personal no less than to social morality the twentieth century has moved into an age of rebellion and revolution against biblical patterns of conduct. The reason for this tendency is found mainly in neglect of the Hebrew-Christian view of God and the world.

The strength of the strategy of *regeneration* lies in this: in contrast to the other modern social philosophies, it flows from the revelation of the Creator-Redeemer God. The biblical message is basically one of supernatural redemption from sin, and the problem of social justice is placed in necessary relationship to man's need and God's provision of

22

salvation. Hence such concepts as the will of God; man's fall; the revealed commandments; the law of love; the prophetic promise of a Redeemer and its fulfillment in Jesus Christ; the need for personal holiness and the gift of the Holy Spirit; the Church as a society of twice-born men and women in union with Christ; the ultimate triumph of the right and the final judgment of the wicked, become central considerations in the Christian approach to the social crisis. Amid the modern crusade for social betterment, therefore, the strategy of *regeneration* proclaims the hard news that social evils contradict man's dignity and destiny by creation, but also the good news of a "new heaven and new earth" assured in Jesus Christ.

3. CONTRASTING DYNAMISMS FOR SOCIAL CHANGE

We do not propose to survey the teachings of the divergent social philosophies; they are many in number and their modifications are legion. Our purpose, rather, has been to see modern movements as competing patterns of social action, relying in turn on their individually peculiar dynamisms for social improvement, and having diverse implications for the Church in its important task of evangelism and missions.

If we ask what dynamic motivates the various social strategies to change the *status quo,* we find a wide range of differences. The strategy of *revolution,* of course, relies on brute power for its promotion of social radicalism: Its upheaval of respected social norms, and substitution of novel forms, depends primarily upon resorting to incendiary methods of force. The *reform* strategy avoids use of violence and intimidation, but for a basic instrument of change relies upon legislated morality, or political compulsion achieved by democratic processess. A generation ago, even before the evolutionary pragmatism of John Dewey invaded the public schools, *reform* looked to public education and moral propaganda to effect social change. In recent decades, however, with the decline of the democracies, *reform* tactics increasingly assume the political complex of Big Government as indispensable to social betterment. Thus social change more and more becomes political action, and government legislation or compulsion the key instrument of such change.

The strategies of *revolution* and *reform* share two fundamental convictions: first, social progress is best secured through a change of social environment; and second, political action most effectively implements this changed evironment. Both strategies neglect spiritual resources to energize moral attitudes and actions; they imply that only governmental compulsion can effectively accomplish benevolent ends. The essential difference between these strategies is that *revolution* aims to achieve its social ends swiftly through violent methods, whereas *reform* seeks to effect them through democratic pressures.

The *revaluation* strategy emphasizes man's spiritual dignity and his superiority to animals and the material world; therefore, it stresses moral education, propaganda, conversation and persuasion as effective media of social change. Its major disagreement with the *revolution* and *reform* strategies is its awareness that merely changed environment without changed human perspective will not effect a fundamental revision of the social situation. *Revaluation* therefore seeks to inculcate an awareness of the religious dimension of life, and to exhibit the significance of the moral man for society and the universe. By stimulating conscience, this strategy relates human rights to human dignity; by stressing man's spiritual value as an individual, it supplies ethical fervor for social change.

The strategy of *regeneration*, by contrast, relies primarily on spiritual dynamic for social change. It aims not merely to re-educate man (although it knows that the Holy Spirit uses truth — particularly the truth of the Gospel — as a means of conviction), but to renew the whole man morally and spiritually through a saving experience of Jesus Christ. The power on which it relies for social change is not totalitarian compulsion, nor is it the power, *per se*, of legislated morality, education, and unregenerate conscience. *Regeneration* rests upon spiritual power. The Gospel of Christ is the Church's peculiar *dynamis* for facing the entire world. Christian social action condones no social solutions in which personal acceptance of Jesus Christ as Saviour and Lord is an optional consideration. Personal regeneration and redemption are inherent in its hope for the social order. It proclaims the Kingdom of God as the new order, not some secular counterpart. And "except a man be born again he cannot see the kingdom of God" (John 3:3). The new birth restores man to fellowship with God, and lifts him not only to the vision of truth and goodness but also qualifies him with a new nature and moral power to place his energies in the service of righteousness. The Holy Spirit sunders the shackles of human sin, requiring men first to recognize social evils in the light of personal wickedness. While personal sin often finds its occasion in the prevailing community situation, the Christian pulpit and personal witness encourage effective solution of social evils by calling out a race of renewed men united in devotion to God's purpose in creation and redemption.

How do other social strategies that rely on competitive means for social change evaluate this peculiar dynamism of religion? *Revolution,* as the Communist pattern discloses full well, scorns supernatural regeneration as a religious fiction. It deliberately "exalts" the natural man and spurns the evangelistic invitation to "the new birth." It impugns evangelical adequacy to confront the social crisis and considers eagerness to repudiate supernaturalistic means as a yardstick of social alertness.

Reform and *revaluation* tactics do not impugn, but nonetheless do disparage, the adequacy or the relevance of divine salvation for the basic social problems of the day. They measure Christian vitality simply by the depth of individual devotion to their own pre-announced social goals. *Revaluation* strategy considers spiritual phenomena congenial instruments to social change, but in energizing moral attitudes and action appeals only to religious resources that are immanent and universally accessible, and not peculiar to the theology of revelation. Its alternative to *regeneration* is moralization of the unregenerate man, and virtual indifference to evangelism and missions.

Supernatural regeneration therefore is the peculiar mainspring for the social metamorphosis latent in the Christian movement. Man's spiritual renewal vitalizes his awareness of God and neighbor, vivifies his senses of morality and duty, fuses the law of love to sanctified compassion, and so registers the ethical impact of biblical religion upon society. Man's personal dispositions are thus enlarged for sacrificial service, and his benevolent desires are qualified by a new moral power. The familiar evangelical call to be "born again," the high task of winning other men to Christ, the pervasive work of the Holy Spirit in sanctification, all contribute to the basic motivations of social impact. Under such divine constraint the believer impresses his influence on society through the family, in immediate neighbor relations, in daily work pursued as a divine vocation, and, as a citizen of two worlds, in fulfillment of civic duties.

Evangelism and revival remain the original wellsprings of evangelical humanitarianism and social awakening. To ignore or lay aside this chief armor of apostolic Christianity for reliance on other social dynamics means retreat from the peculiar glory of the New Testament to the world-wisdom and world-power of the Greeks and Romans. Those who in social agitation sponsor a morality of compulsion, or simply trust the word and will of unregenerate men, thereby betray their skepticism of the adequacy of spiritual reserves latent in the Christian religion. This gnawing doubt is manifest in the notion that social problems are not wholly responsive to spiritual solutions. Consequently, the Church has often turned aside from its evangelistic and missionary priorities, attempting to chart a socio-political thrust *alongside* rather than *in* and *through* the evangelistic thrust. Such direct engagement of the Church in politics and economics when it relies on earthly endowments and energies alone, has no biblical mandate. It neglects the Gospel's relevance and indispensability to the whole of the Church's work, including its mission to society.

4. CONTRASTING VIEWS OF THE CHURCH

Communism rightly senses an intrinsic connection between the Church and its distinctive supernatural dynamic, and therefore rejects both. The Church may be tolerated now and then for strategic purposes, especially if it confines itself to private piety and morality. Indeed, it may even be humored if it co-operates in promoting revolutionary social changes. Whenever the Church remains the Church, however, Communism quickly calls it reactionary, charging it with moral turpitude in the face of "social inequalities."

The *reform* strategy is less extreme. It may deplore sluggish conscience in the churches, but seldom does it decry the existence of the Church itself as an historical phenomenon. *Reform* strategy still values churches as influences for social idealism, and even more, as latent pressure blocs for social action. Reform agitators discount the importance of church affiliation, but prize whatever churches do to promote approved socio-political changes. The reason for this *reform* attitude is clear: its program of social betterment does not look to the churches for any significant reservoirs of moral energy. So, too, with the strategy of *revaluation*. Churches may indeed be specially concerned centers of community

27

action that could hold the balance of moral power if once aroused to the social task. But the conviction seems to remain that the central dynamic for social impact does not derive from the churches. Many social pioneers in the *revaluation* movement support and encourage independent programs, and even establish operations competitive to the Church. Many have left the pulpit ministry to co-ordinate such enterprises outside the Church, and point with gratification to those other ecclesiastical leaders who support them while remaining in the Church. But the Church itself is no longer honored and recognized as the authentic bearer of a revealed social ethic.

Christ founded neither a party of revolutionaries, nor a movement of reformers, nor a remnant of revaluators. He "called out a people." The twice-born fellowship of his redeemed Church, in vital company with its Lord, alone mirrored the realities of the new social order. This new order was no mere distant dream, waiting for the proletariat to triumph, or the evolutionary process to reach its pinnacle, or truth to win its circuitous way throughout the world. In a promissory way the new order had come *already* in Jesus Christ and in the regenerate fellowship of his Church. The Lord was ascended; he reigned over all. Hence the apostolic Church would not yield to other rulers or to other social visions. It could not obey some earthly leader, covet some power other than the Gospel, or reverence some man-made commission. The Christian Church knew Jesus Christ. He furnished the spiritual resources for its moral confrontation of the world. From his throne in the eternal order the Living Head mediated to the Body an earnest of the powers that belong to the age to come. This earnest or sample was adequate to turn the apostolic age right side up.

It will not be amiss to call to mind the verdict of two distinguished historians over the social impact of biblical Christianity. Writing of the early centuries, W. E. H. Lecky had this to say: "The greatest religious change in the history of mankind" took place "under the eyes of a brilliant galaxy of philosophers and historians" who disregarded "as simply contemptible an agency which all men must now admit to have been . . . the most powerful moral lever that has ever been applied to the affairs of men."[3] And the church historian F. J. Foakes-Jackson, with an eye on recent times (after conceding — as every impartial chronicler must — that "no branch indeed of the Western Church can be refused the honor of having assisted in the progress of humane ideas, and non-Christians have participated largely in the work of diffusing the modern spirit of kindness"), reminds us that "the credit of the inception of the movement belongs without doubt to that of Protestantism which is distinguished by the importance it attaches to the doctrine of the Atonement . . . . History shows that the thought of Christ on the Cross has been more potent than anything else in arousing a compassion for suffering and indignation at injustice . . . . The later Evangelicalism, which saw in the death of Christ the means of free salvation for fallen humanity, caused its adherents to take the front rank as champions of the weak. . . . Prison reform, the prohibition of the slave trade, the abolition of slavery, the Factory Acts, the protection of children, the crusade against cruelty to animals, are all the outcome of the great evangelical revival of the eighteenth century. The humanitarian tendencies of the nineteenth century, which, it is but just to admit all Christian communities have fostered, and which non-Christian philanthropists have vied with them in encouraging, are among the greatest triumphs of the power and influence of Christ."[4]

So a regard for the history of the West, from apostolic

---

[3] W. H. Lecky, *History of European Morals* (New York: D. Appleton, 1905), I, 388.

[4] F. J. Foakes-Jackson, "Christ in the Church," in H. B. Swete (ed.), *Cambridge Theological Essays* (New York: Macmillan, 1905), pp. 512-514.

times to the modern era, channels the concern for social transformation to the evangelical movement and calls the turbulent modern era anew to those spiritual dynamisms to which the Bible pays its sustained witness. The Christian movement has a stake — a vital stake — in education and legislation. It need not disparage every effort at reform and revaluation as abortively competitive, aware though it is that only the sounder capital borrowed from earlier evangelical influences preserves much of this current interest in a changed society from bankruptcy. Yet Christianity knows — and it dare not forget nor let the world forget — that what the social order most needs is a new race of men — men equipped not simply with new textbooks and new laws, but with new hearts.

II. THE CHRISTIAN VIEW OF WORK

A DISTINCTIVE FEATURE OF NEW TESTAMENT ETHICS IS ITS call to every believer to serve God and neighbor. Within family and community redeemed man stands in social relationship to both divine and human society. This dual relationship motivates his social responsibilities and by it he is linked to the whole enterprise of civilization.

The believer may indeed neglect his political or civic duties, and may evade his stake in education. But since the Christian as well as the non-Christian must work to eat, he must therefore engage in economic pursuits and enter into relationships engendered by his daily work, relationships as spontaneous and normal as his more private involvements. In commuting between the intimate circle of the family and the larger family of society, employer and employee alike are summoned to use their talents for the good of others. According to the scriptural perspective, work becomes a way-station of spiritual witness and service, a daily-traveled bridge between theology and social ethics. In other words, work for the believer is a sacred stewardship, and in fulfilling his job he will either accredit or violate the Christian witness. When viewed as a priestly ministry, man's labors thus become "good works" that radiate from a spiritually dedicated life.

Christianity has undoubtedly given new vigor and dignity to the belittled world of work. With its penetration of the pagan West, the Christian religion etched a halo, as it were, around man's daily labor. Instead of being just a time-consuming routine, a drab, monotonous sparring for subsistence devoid of ultimate meaning and laden only with burden and uncertainty, the workaday world was now interpreted as a divinely appointed sphere where man as a worker is ordained to glorify God, and in His name to serve his fellow man. Upon the humblest carpenter shop Christianity bestowed something of the radiance of Nazareth; through the tired limbs of even the lowliest slave the Gospel sent a surge of glory.

This unique sense of meaning and value is all but gone from today's panorama of labor. Employers and employees alike admit that something has gone awry. Management is hard put to find trustworthy workers, and statesmen lament a lack of reliable aides. But these executives and diplomats themselves exemplify the working world's futility; their own activities disclose the same lack of mission and meaning as do those of dockhands and electricians.

If the daily job is no longer the most time-*consuming* aspect of human existence, it has nonetheless for countless thousands become life's most time-*oppressive* factor. Today the hours "on the job" are like a grievous, unending plague. Even with the shortened work week — from forty-eight to forty-four to forty hours — perhaps even, more conspicuously where workers propagandize for thirty-five — men remain restive and disgruntled under the crushing weight of time. Hours seem like interminable days, days like unending weeks. Even many a housewife suggests this same emptiness of challenge by her monotonous assembly line of ten-minute frozen pastries, three-minute soups and thirty-second waffles. Once an outdoor sun dial was sufficient to subdivide the daily hours. Now we need clocks in every room and memo books of every size to apportion our daily, weekly, monthly, and yearly commitments. Much as he may grumble about punching the tyrannical time clock on the job, the modern man sports his self-winding, shock- and waterproof calendar wrist watch that by the minute, even by the second, relentlessly mirrors the predicament of his unmotivated life. This zooming from one split second to another (whatever blessings modern conveniences may have brought) discloses an unwitting modern paradox of our day: we dread its barrenness, yet enslave ourselves to the crowding of time.

As if by way of compensation, the worker tries to crowd a new dimension into his "off the job" existence. He fights time by hurrying through his meals, through his leisure, and even through his sleep. The haunting emptiness of the working hours drives him to find some meaning for life at other levels of time consumption. Since far too often he shuns the religious dimension of life, he slights the biblical cycle of "work and rest (worship)" with its focus on sin and redemption. If he does exhibit religious curiosity, his mood (since the regular churches do little to reach the worker anyway) makes him an easy target for mystic cults that declare time to be an "illusion" and promise him some kind of ecstatic absorption into the timeless infinite. More likely, the worker turns first to leisure, and usually to a kind that has corrupted its capacity for genuine *re*creation. He may reach for escape in the romanticism or cynicism of all kinds and levels of reading, or in the vivid sensualism of the stage and theatre. But his leisure is impotent to compensate for the forfeiture of worship and the meaninglessness of work. He may try to lose himself in drink, in sexual indulgence, even in narcotics. Sometimes he chooses suicide as the only answer to his misery. Without spiritual orientation, time "off the job" soon becomes just as futile as time "on the job." When man loses the sacred significance of work and of himself as worker, he soon loses the sacred meaning of time and of life.

For this reason a religion or philosophy which fails to grapple with the seeming meaninglessness of work seldom challenges the modern worker. To warn against Marxism's dismissal of religion as "the opiate of the masses" is needful, but unless a religion or philosophy discovers ultimate meaning and worth in the world of work, it will gain little hearing and exercise little social power. Whether they want to or not, most adults — including the overwhelming majority of church members — spend most of their conscious lives in the world of work. Unless a man's religion maintains relevance for him beyond Sunday into all his weekday pursuits, it soon forfeits its spiritual significance for him. If the Church yields his work and leisure to secularism, and asks him to reserve only prayer meeting or Sunday services for God, then it erodes the biblical concept of Christian commitment that encompasses the vast oceanfront of secular concerns to but a tiny, inadequate beachhead of private devotion. Such limited religious penetration has nothing further to say to the worker beyond counsel against addicition to vices like gambling and liquor. As Dorothy Sayers has said in *Creed or Chaos*, the plea is to "come to church and avoid drink and disorderly conduct." In short, unless the Church makes a difference in a Simon Peter's pursuits at the *fish*-level, the Christian "life" becomes simply another "extra" among his items of work and play. If Christian commitment does not integrate and govern the totality of life, the worker soon comes to regard it as just another extraneous, perhaps superfluous adjunct to his already cumbersome work week. According to Alexander Miller, "the growing alienation of workers from the Church — virtually complete in Britain, increasing in North America"[1] comes from the laborer's sense that "church can only be for those who are not soiled with the sordid work of the world."[1]

Communism seized the propaganda value of this sorry state of affairs by ascribing labor's feeling of frustration to the capitalist system. It proclaimed that capitalism inherently

[1] Alexander Miller, *Christian Faith and My Job* (New York: Association Press, 1946), p. 10.

depreciates and exploits the working class. Promising instead a new world order that "glorifies" the worker, Communism soon quickened the lagging spirit of the laborer. If performed with thoroughgoing loyalty to "the Party" and with a view to the coming world revolution, even the most menial task now gained larger social significance. The worker thus joined a cause "wide as the world," one that promised the nobility and romance of personal recognition.

Today disappointed multitudes in the Communist bloc, and peoples of the Free World as well, recognize this Marxist distortion for what it is. The collectivistic promise of status for the worker has become a tragic mirage. Not the worker, but his hard work, is glorified. Vyacheslov Molotov illustrated this fact in remarks at the Stakhanovite conference of 1936: "Counting minutes and seconds during one's work introduces a rhythm . . . means introducing culture in one's work. It is therefore not a question of overstrain on the part of the worker but a culture attitude toward work."[2] The worker becomes merely a tool whose highest good is whole-souled subserviency to the totalitarian state. Instead of being glorified, the worker is demeaned and degraded as a political mechanism.

1. The Recognition of Work as a Calling

However appalling this situation may be, Communism could not have lured the worker to this "glorification" unless he had previously surrendered the biblical vision of the dedication and sanctification of work. Capitulation was even simpler in the Orient, where the relatively small influence of Christian missions had lifted the sense of futility very little. Pagan religions in fact underscored the feeling of disdain for this life and temporal concerns. With no

---

[2] As quoted in Arthur Koestler, *The Yogi and the Commissar* (New York: Macmillan, 1945), p. 162.

concept of honoring the Living God in and through their daily work, the Asian and African were ready prey for Communism's supposed romanticizing of labor. This Marxist fiction could not have intrigued Western man but for his ignorance or perversion of the Christian view of work. And, indeed, this decline actually began long before Communism's outright repudiation of Christian supernaturalism. With waning success the West had struggled, first against the Medieval church's faulty interpretation of work, and then more recently against modern dilutions of the biblical ideal.

It was the Roman Catholic misconception of vocation that prepared the way for the gradual inroads of modern secularism upon the Christian view of work. In the Middle Ages and throughout the centuries, Rome limited the idea of vocation only to the priestly class. By placing the monk in a special life of isolation and rigorous self-discipline, monastic Christianity also limited the meaning of "vocation." Even today the *Catholic Encyclopedia* restricts the term "vocation" to priests, monks, and nuns, while the Jesuit abbreviation S.J. (Society of Jesus) suggests that one cannot fully follow Jesus outside the priesthood. In other words, Catholicism regards only the priestly class, and not the laity, as being in the service of God.

Such denial of the priesthood of all believers has two important consequences: it excludes the laity from divine service, and it elevates the priesthood above the world of labor. To be both a laborer and a priest, or to be both a priest and a laborer, is impossible in Catholicism, for to unite both tasks in one person is to nullify the Roman concept of the priesthood. This bifurcation was dramatized recently when papal strictures were levelled against French "worker-priests" who had put aside clerical habits to work alongside factory laborers in order to win them back to the church and away from Communist encroachment. To remove the clergy from the world of labor, and to preclude the laity from service of God, as Romanism has done, actually yields an incomplete, even perverted definition of vocation. It was this unjustifiable disjunction which led to the divorce of the sacred from the secular and denied manual and non-ecclesiastical work the significance of divine "calling" or "vocation." Participation in the social order and in the world of trade, while admittedly proper and legitimate, was considered distinctly less honorable than the priestly life of seclusion and celibacy; only the world-isolated and world-insulated life of monk or nun, said the Medieval church, can be truly religious.

This declaration the Protestant Reformation thoroughly renounced. But perhaps because it did not fully grasp the significance of this repudiation, the fundamentalist movement modified the Catholic concept of vocation only partially. Even so, fundamentalism's understanding of Christian vocation was still more incisive than that of the religious humanism and Protestant liberalism (much of it anti-supernaturalistic) that pervaded the twentieth century. These latter movements largely left the philosophy and exposition of work to labor reformers whose thinking arose from modern, often socialistic or quasi-socialistic, economic theories rather than from sound biblical principles. The term "vocation," thus totally secularized, came to be merely a synonym for occupational preference. Work became only a means of livelihood for oneself and one's dependents, and material gain its chief goal. Except possibly for avoidance of grossly wicked pursuits, the laborer detached the idea of work entirely from any religious reference.

Vocational guidance tests, respected as virtually omni-competent, are now trusted to provide a reliable outside source of direction. Their scores determine not only an individual's natural gifts and dispositions, but also the best choice of career for the greatest measure of personal success and satisfaction. Ironically enough, the profession that popularized guidance tests has produced some rather startling statistics concerning itself. Recent surveys contend that among school teachers thirty per cent are emotionally and socially maladjusted; at least ten per cent need psychiatric help; one in ten teachers has had a nervous breakdown. The efficacy of aptitude tests is undergoing investigation by various sources. Several Columbia professors, in fact, have conceded that they could not determine whether a candidate would make a better doctor than lawyer. There is growing recognition, too, that such time-tested traits as ambition, efficiency and responsibility — virtues that the Reformation stressed in its contribution to capitalism — are just as vital for success as some other less abstract factors. Furthermore, vocational screening has no device for anticipating spiritual influences, such as the impetus given to neglected abilities by a religious motivation, or the shaping of new talents for new tasks to which the Spirit directs obedient believers.

However helpful this work orientation may be, it is still fundamentally secular. It takes no cognizance of "divine calling." In fact, the ministry (pastor or missionary) that lays claim only to such motivation ekes out an uneasy respect. Religious humanism thinks only in terms of social service (secular antitype of divine service), and tends to confer a suspect cult-status on careers that insist upon supernatural constraint. But while humanism intentionally secularized work, seeking nonetheless to impart ethical overtones to what it had stripped of supernatural sanction, Protestant liberalism secularized it unwittingly. The idealistic school made all work a "ministry" in its own way; to promote social conscience, it appealed to the unselfish brotherhood or neighbor-love of Jesus of Nazareth. Through its pantheistic Absolute, idealism reinforced "my station and its duties" for everyone. Liberalism's preoccupation with the social gospel, however, along with its neglect of the Great Commission, cuts the foundation from under a specially called and commissioned

ministry. While humanism, therefore, deliberately secularized
the sphere of work (since a purely time-bound world yields
everything to transient significance), liberalism equalized all
pursuits by surrendering "the glory of the ministry" and
by neglecting the overall biblical view of vocation. This
change of perspective resulted not only in the mere moraliz-
ing of labor but supplied a first step toward decline of the
ministry in prestige among the professions. In many ministerial
homes the second generation came for wrong reasons to
prefer social work or State Department service to the pulpit.

As already suggested, the evangelical reaction represented
more a revision of the Roman Catholic and secular views
than a full recovery of the apostolic and Reformation doctrine
of vocation. To be sure, it repudiated the Catholic idea of
a separate priestly class and insisted, with the Reformers,
on the priesthood of all believers. And against liberalism, the
evangelical movement defended the concept of a special
divine call to technical vocational service in the proclamation
of miraculous divine redemption. But it failed to delineate
the Reformation thesis that every believer's daily work is to
minister to God and man. Fundamentalism blended aspects
of the Catholic, Reformation, and secular approaches. And it
did raise the question whether, in addition to an ordained
ministry and missionary task force, God calls some believers
to specific vocations. But although it recognized areas of
special Christian service and of evangelical calling (particularly teaching and medicine, if not law, since these were
tied directly to enterprises of Christian education and missions), fundamentalism hesitated to relate divine calling to
every type of work. By linking "decision for full-time Christian service" (quite apart from the question or ordination)
to a few select activities, it implied that other types of
work are necessarily secular. A letter from Christ for Greater
Los Angeles, Inc., supplies a telling example. As one of
the most gratifying "decisions" of the Harbor Crusade, the

letter tells of a U.S. Marine bound for law school who, upon conversion, decided to enter the ministry instead. We are not disputing the high calling of the ministry, but rather the apparent rejection of law as a Christian vocation. The letter's question, "Who can measure the result of that one decision . . . ?" could easily imply that the will of God precludes evangelical dedication in the field of law.

It must be granted that the fundamentalist movement sought to impart spiritual overtones to occupational activity. Every believer was to identify himself as a Christian by refraining from morally questionable work — such as the liquor traffic and gambling enterprises (even if permitted by law). Certain tasks such as public school teaching were singled out as offering fuller scope for indirect witness or secondary service to the Church. If possible, moreover, Christians were to find fellowship as workers in organizations like the Christian Business Men's Committee, the Christian Business and Professional Women's Club, and so on. They should bear glad witness about the forgiveness of sins to be found through Jesus Christ; they should avoid laziness on the job, and shoddy business ethics; they should maintain a reputation for integrity, punctuality, courtesy, co-operation, dependability, and diligence (cf. Prov. 6:6-11; 12:24, 27; 13:11; 14:23; 18:9; 22:29; 24:30-34; Eccl. 9:10).

Still, fundamentalism did not comprehend all work as divine vocation, as spiritual service to God and man. The subject of "divine vocation" was table talk only in the parsonage or at missionary society headquarters. Must a person who is a "born" musician, artist, writer, or politician also be divinely "called" to such pursuits? This fact explains the embarrassing lack, for example, of evangelical journalists, authors, and playwrights who might be strategically useful to the religious enterprise in an era of mass communication. Church memberships include many gifted persons whose first-rate talents are spiritually undedicated.

For this reason many of the most crucial posts in today's economic world remain beyond the claim of Christian vocation, and accordingly are abandoned to non-Christian motivations and ideals. To integrate Sunday worship with weekday work becomes an ever-enlarging problem. The question continues to be asked: How shall or can the believer exist in the steel mills of Pittsburgh, the oil fields of Tulsa, the auto factories of Detroit, the shopping districts of New York and all the while remain a citizen of heaven? Even in evangelical churches, contractors and plasterers, tailors and truckdrivers, secretaries and domestics seem unable to identify their work in terms of "divine calling." Perhaps this absence of evangelical challenge to workers at the labor level explains why the evangelistic thrust has found so little response among the laboring class as such, and especially among organized labor, whose activities are dictated so largely by secular organizations.

Through the New Testament concept of the believer's calling to a life of service, the early Christians had recognized the dignity of man's labor over against the pagan view of work. Albert C. Knudson's surmise, that because of eschatological anticipations the early Christians were not much influenced by the concept of vocational calling, is groundless.[3] Paul uses hope in the return of Christ to reinforce the high view of vocation, and criticizes those who are tempted to ignore it (I Thess. 4:11f.).

By "calling" the New Testament means primarily an invitation to accept Christ. This invitation is inwardly prompted by the Spirit of God and is voiced outwardly usually through the preaching of the Gospel. The meaning of "calling" involves more, however. God's purpose in "calling" attaches a horizontal as well as vertical dimension

[3] Albert C. Knudson, *Principles of Christian Ethics* (New York & Nashville: Abingdon-Cokesbury, 1943), ch. 9.

to the believer's life (Rom. 11:29; Phil. 3:14; Eph. 1:18; 4:1; II Tim. 1:9; II Pet. 1:10), a concept already implicit in the teaching of love toward neighbor. Believers are exhorted to "walk worthy" of their "vocation" (Eph. 4:1, KJV; ARV and RV, "calling"). In I Corinthians 7:20, Paul uses the term for man's entire station in life; his earthly calling encompasses nothing less than his total life situation, all social involvements included. The believer's whole life is a mission "in the Lord"; hence if any activity whatsoever in his life becomes secular in its orientation, the believer's calling is profaned. The scriptural definition of "calling" makes no distinction between sacred and secular.

The Bible doctrine of work goes still deeper. The Old Testament already gave clear evidence of individuals being called not only as priests and prophets, but also as workmen in other specific areas of activity (Exod. 31:2-11; Isa. 22: 20). By insisting on the universal priesthood of believers, the New Testament implies the necessity of doing any and all work as a spiritual service.

But not until the Protestant Reformation did a fully developed concept of vocation become apparent. This Reformation-acquired meaning of *vocatio* Max Weber emphasizes in his *General Economic History*.[4] Luther used the German word *Beruf* (calling) in a sense overlooked by the Catholics, and employed it even to translate the Greek word *ponos* (toil). Like Calvin, he represented vocation as an avenue of divine service, although his view lacked Calvin's profundity. Luther indeed denied the superiority of monastic labor, and emphasized that man's calling is to be fulfilled not in a monastery but in the world. But he did not elaborate the implications of obedience and resignation to God's will for man's particular situation and duty. Calvin, on the other hand, dignified the occupation of all workers in terms

4 New York: Greenberg, 1927.

of a divine calling that moves them beyond obedience to active outgoing service. As Henry J. Ryskamp puts it, "Whereas Calvin exhorted his readers and followers to serve God *through* their vocations, Luther was content with the idea that men should not neglect to serve God *in* their vocations . . . ."[5] Yet Luther told his followers: "God even milks the cows through you," and restored to man's work the music that Christianity first put into the working man's heart. English fishermen and Russian harvesters often broke into song as they labored. And in Iowa, American farmers had a saying that even the cows knew the difference when a dairyman was converted.

Over against Rome's distinction between the religious and the secular, which granted spiritual merit only to those in specifically designated religious pursuits, the Reformers insisted that every believer's calling is sacred. The Reformation intention, as Alexander Miller notes, was not to do away with all priests, but rather "to make all Christians priests."[6] The layman has a calling in Christ no less than the minister, and the daily labor of both, performed as a consecrated sacrifice, is equally acceptable as spiritual service. On this basis, Martin Luther is said to have liberated not only the monks in the monasteries but all men to fulfill their divine vocation. The Reformation did not eliminate the priesthood but rather did away with a non-priestly laity; every follower of Jesus Christ was reminded anew of his calling to full-time priestly service. This emphasis did not so much secularize the ministry as it sanctified the laity. The Christian workman becomes a priest among his fellow-workers; he serves both God and neighbor by offering God the labor of his hands as a daily sacrifice. D. Elton Trueblood

5 Henry J. Ryskamp, "Calvinistic Action and Modern Economic Patterns," in Clarence Bouma, *et al., God-Centered Living* (Grand Rapids, Mich.: Baker, 1951), p. 182.

6 Miller, *op. cit.,* p. 27.

has aptly remarked that, whereas the Reformation came when the Bible was opened for the minister, the twentieth century resurgence will come when the ministry is opened for the layman.

The Reformation, as we have said, viewed every calling as sacred, and work as a medium in and through which the believer offers himself to God. Life's variety of callings implies no distinction in the respective value or dignity of those engaged therein; God's purpose in the calling is the discriminating factor and not man's superiority or inferiority. God is served by obedience, not by self-chosen vocations (cf. Isa. 1:11-17; Hos. 6:6; Matt. 9:13; 12:7); no gift, whether mental or physical, is genuinely *devoted* to society except in and through the "call." Faithful obedience to God's call makes the clergy as good as, but no better than, the devout merchant or shoemaker. Similarly, God expects the gardener or grocer to perform his labor as a spiritual service just as fully as the minister. As Christ was faithful in his calling, so all men are to be faithful in theirs. Thus our Lord's "Go ye into all the world" anticipated the extension of his lordship not only by the preaching of the Gospel as such, but also by his claim on the world of work — the world of finance, law, education, science, politics, and all else. While posts and places of service are different, all believers have the very same call, namely, to be in Christ; through this call all labor gains new dignity as a field of spiritual service.

If work is defined as the service of God, some pursuits obviously are not legitimate callings, particularly those which come from or support other men's sins. In such cases, not even the pressure of circumstances excuses the Christian; since he cannot thank God for such perverted work, he cannot define it as a divine vocation. "He that followeth me shall not walk in darkness," said Jesus (John 8:12). The activities of shame cannot therefore be reconciled with divine call. The criminal, dope-peddler, professional prostitute or bookie, demonstrate ignorance of the meaning of vocation, and also of the meaning of salvation. Whatever inherently lowers the spiritual and moral appetites of men cannot be made holy. It is difficult to see how the believer can work in gambling enterprises, either as owner, employee, or investor, or be allied with large areas of today's entertainment world. God wills for the Christian a good work; therefore the Christian must desert the service of sin and Satan (cf. Heb. 13:21). Sometimes, in the absence of other means of livelihood, believers have been forced into work which they cannot pursue with undefiled conscience. It is a tragic mistake, then, if the Church simply watches from the sidelines and condemns. To find legitimate avenues for investing God-given talents should be a concern of the spiritual community; the employed should help bear the burdens of the unemployed by suggesting legitimate work opportunities and by assisting them financially, lest talents be perverted and the Lord dishonored. Insofar as energy expended for economic reward is honorable, and genuinely dignified as work, it is to be conceived in terms of spiritual calling.

Every time the Christian worker leaves his home for work, he moves from the private social sphere of the family to the public sphere of labor and economics. Through the Christian on the job the world meets the Church. But it meets far more: it meets the Divine Worker. To what extent the worker understands the biblical doctrine of vocation will be demonstrated by his work-attitude and work-accomplishment, by how he answers the question: "What difference does Christianity make in my job?" Is his work simply a means of subsistence, self-discipline and character development (I Thess. 4:11,12; II Thess. 3:11), or is it the provision of God, to be fulfilled as an expression of worship by dedicating God-given talents to the Lord's service and to mankind? Is his labor only a means of developing bodily and mental powers by yielding to the orderly necessities of work, or is it an investment of personality in response to God's ordinance and calling? Is daily work recognized as a religious duty and practice, as an opportunity for divine service? Does the worker demonstrate the certainty that vocational talents are an endowment not basically for selfish use, nor even for the sake of society as such, but for the service of the Saviour and His will for man and the world? Does this religious commitment permeate the decision-making and strength-consuming aspects of his hours on the job? Whether he be manufacturer, merchant, or salesman, the believer in and through his vocation becomes steeped in the social task. To neglect such a call is to contribute to the deterioration and distintegration of society, and the undedicated worker therefore becomes guilty of ethical disobedience.

For the Christian, then, this spiritual dedication heads the list of those principles which determine his choice and fulfillment of work; it takes precedence over other factors such as salary, opportunity for advancement, working conditions, and so on. If work is primarily a means of service, and of self-giving, it ceases to be primarily a means of acquisition; that is, its chief end is not money-making. If talents are recognized as a divine gift, a man's performance of that for which he is best suited is more important to an employee than searching for the highest pay and more important to the employer than searching for the cheapest labor. The believer's prime interest, under God, will be in good work that promotes human good.

2. THE BIBLE AND THE DIGNITY OF WORK

In contrast to those who debase work as an unfortunate alternative to leisure, or simply as necessary to subsistence or to material comfort and gain, biblical religion stresses

THE CHRISTIAN VIEW OF WORK

the high dignity of work in various ways. It affirms, among other things, that:

(1) *God's purpose in creation maintains the dignity of work.* Under God his Maker, man is to exercise dominion over the earth, a dominion which centers in the intelligible, ethical, and spiritual direction of the world's affairs.

Created in the spiritual and moral image of God (Gen. 1:26-28), man's larger vocation is to rule the earth in obedience to the Ruler of all things. By creation man is assigned a distinctive task on this planet: "Be fruitful, and multiply, and replenish the earth, and subdue it: and have dominion over the fish of the sea, and over the fowl of the air, and over every living thing that moveth upon the earth" (Gen. 1:28). In Erich Sauer's words, "The extending of man's rule on earth, provided he remain subject to God, signified a drawing of all things earthly into the sphere of the moral world-purposes . . . . Paradise was thus the fixed point from which the uplifting of Nature into the sphere of the spirit should take its beginning . . . . The Paradise garden is beginning and end, start and goal, basis, programme, and type of the whole task of man on earth."[7] This earthly dominion God allotted neither to the angels nor to the higher animals, but rather to the human race, whose task becomes, in consequence, the spiritual control of the earth. Man is to achieve this dominion by inhabiting the earth and by subjugating nature. Human nature is intended not simply to supplement but also to lift the physical and animal worlds to their proper function under God.

The Bible nowhere depicts human labor as a result of the Fall. According to the creation account, the Creator assigned work to man even before sin entered. Adam was given a specific task that involved a work relationship both

[7] Erich Sauer, *The Dawn of World Redemption* (London: Paternoster Press, 1951), pp. 45f.

47

to God and to the world: "And the Lord God took the man, and put him into the garden of Eden to dress it and to keep it. And the Lord God commanded the man . . . " (Gen. 2:15f.). Since the Protestant Reformers oriented man's daily work to God's original purpose for mankind, and resisted its delineation in the context of sin, Albert C. Knudson rightly remarked that "it was the reformation that released work from the curse of the fall . . . and represented it as a divine order of creation."[8]

Through his work, man thus shares the creation-purpose of God in subduing nature, whether he be a miner with dirty hands, a mechanic with greasy face, or a stenographer with stencil-smudged fingers. Work is permeated by purpose; it is intended to serve God, benefit mankind, make nature subservient to the moral program of creation. Man must therefore apply his whole being — heart and mind, as well as hand — to the daily job. As God's fellow-worker he is to reflect God's creative activity on Monday in the factory no less than on Sunday when commemorating the day of rest and worship.

To consider work a channel of divine creation, by which the creature serves God and man, carries certain consequences for one's attitude toward labor. The Christian becomes morally obligated to withhold producing, and even purchasing (since money is the conversion of his talent into cash) culturally worthless, let alone wicked and harmful, items. Nor will he engage in their promotion or distribution. As Treglown remarks, "There can be no sense of purpose in making trash."[9] In this regard, the Church has sensed too little its potentially constructive impact on industry; it has not fully sensitized the conscience of the Christian worker to God's purpose for human labor on the basis of creation.

8 Knudson, *op. cit.,* p. 272.
9 G. L. Treglown, *The Christian and His Daily Work* (London: Epworth Press, 1952), p. 15.

(2) *God's example maintains the dignity of work.* Every convert to Christianity has had some exposure to the truths of divine creation, preservation, and redemption. Few believers, however, sense the uniqueness among the world's religions of its doctrine concerning the "works of God." This commonplace of every course in systematic theology, which considers first the nature and then the work of God, points up a remarkable dissimilarity between the Hebrew-Christian religion and other theological views of antiquity.

The classicism of Greece contained no doctrine of divine creation, of revelation and redemption, or of the works of God. To these Greek philosophers, God was an infinite Thinker but not a Worker — a concept, obviously, which had far-reaching consequences for the pagan view of work. Related to their concept of God was the Greek supposition that matter is both eternal and evil. And because of matter's supposed eternity, God could be architect but not creator of the world. But even if he could be architect, the Greeks still hesitated to speak of God as being at work. Plato's artificer-God, or Demiurge, did indeed fashion the immortal parts of the world, but he left the grosser more "mundane" details to inferior deities. Perhaps Plato believed that God would soil his hands with brute stuff. Aristotle's God is even more remote: his only activity is self-thinking thought.

As with the gods, so with men: thinking is nobler than manual labor, according to the Greeks. Moreover, these activities differentiate two classes of men, namely the philosopher or man of leisure, and the slave destined for the menial tasks of life. This tendency to disparage non-intellectual pursuits is already evident in Egypt as early as the time of Israel's sojourn. When the Egyptians, who disdained agricultural pursuits, discovered that the Hebrews were an agricultural people, they assigned the captives to the distant land of Goshen, where the Jews soon were in bondage.

49

The essential contast in attitude between biblical and pagan views of work is evident even from language patterns. While the Old Testament concedes and adjusts to the fact of slavery as a circumstance of those times, the Hebrew theocracy had no linguistic term to distinguish between one class of humans as slaves (in the strict sense) and another as hired servants. Both are designated by the one Hebrew term *ebed* (laborer or worker), a term which quite naturally then comes to be used for a servant. Indeed, the description "servant of God" was applied to Moses and other great Hebrew leaders as a title of honor, not of degradation. The Hebrew religion saw no reason to apologize for the circumstance that Saul and David, its great kings, had been shepherds, and had come to the throne from the flock and the field. While Hebrew conscience protested against anything that rendered work oppressive, it found nothing degrading in work as such. The Messiah, whom David prefigured, later called himself the Good Shepherd, and unhesitatingly defended his redemptive mission by declaring: "My Father worketh hitherto, and I work" (John 5:17).

Man as a worker finds his archtype in God the mighty Worker. Think of God's mighty works. The Great Worker, "*maker* of heaven and earth" (Apostles' Creed), created out of nothing (whereas man takes what God has already fashioned and, at best, reshapes it by combination and recombination). God made the light, the heavens and earth, the stars, the birds and beasts, then man in his own image for fellowship with himself. What magnificent power! What matchless skill! What superb artistry! Think of what was "all in a day's work" for the Almighty One! We read of his labor on the "First day," "Second day," "Third day," and so on. Whether by "day" the narrator of Genesis intended literal days or ages is uncertain. But he stuns us with the recital of God's works.

Work actually reveals one's inner being or character. This

fact is as true of a magistrate, a taxi driver, or a typist, as it is of the Creator and Redeemer of the universe. Just think what God's work discloses about his nature! Behind his work is the activity of a great intelligence. God's universe reflects order and progress. Behind this space-time world is a majestic Planner.

But behind God's world is more than a Planner; there is a Preserver. The universe he has called into existence God sustains. He stands by his work; he does not abandon it. There is no "moral holiday," no unjustifiable strike, no premature retirement. The history of both ecclesiastical movements and local churches is studded with leaders whose energies flagged when it came to preserving the promising programs they originated. The work of God does not stop with creation; it includes preservation.

Behind God's world is still more than a Planner and Preserver; there is a Lover. God is not only a Creator, but also a Redeemer. The hands that shaped our destiny are nail-scarred, scarred not by chance or accident, but by foreordained, redemptive love.

Work gains its dignity, therefore, from the example of God the Creator, Sustainer, and Redeemer of man and the world. This Divine Worker man is to reflect in himself as a worker. He is to mirror God as thinker, willer, redeemer. His human labor is to reflect the divine romance of deity in action. There is something godlike in the projection of a plan, in the articulation of a creative idea, in the giving of oneself to a task. Man's work discloses who it is that works — what nature of thinker, of willer, of lover.

(3) *The example of Jesus Christ, the carpenter of Nazareth, maintains the dignity of work.* The tiny village of Nazareth must have been dotted with the nail-studded creations of those very hands which later were crudely hammered to the tree, for the promised Messiah of Hebrew-Christian religion spent his years as a youth at work in a

carpenter shop. Today, no matter where men may speak of The Carpenter of Nazareth, he is identified at once. This phase of Jesus' active obedience is too often neglected (even in the standard "Lives" of Christ). Christ hallowed the concept of vocation; he incorporated the activities of the workaday world into God's purpose for his life. Day after day, not simply for the space of three years, but for many years, he handled tools and did so to the constant glory of God. It was said of him when he was the Carpenter of Nazareth that he "grew in favor with God and man" (Luke 2:52). It is inconceivable that he would consider his daily task a chore and not a challenge; that he should be content with shoddy and disreputable work instead of showing himself a master craftsman. He whose creative Word hewed all things out of nothing, whose redemptive work shaped a means of escape for sin-doomed man, and who in the judgment to come will "lay the axe to the tree," took the measure of material things in Nazareth just as he would in time take the measure of sinful man and make all things new.

What do we learn from the Son of God in the Nazareth workshop? For one thing, he teaches us that it is possible to be his disciple and to glorify God at a factory bench or on the assembly line. Jesus can and does endorse labor. As V. Raymond Edman remarks in *Storms and Starlight*, "Work has been forever dignified and hallowed by the head and heart and hands of the Lord Jesus." The handling of tools need not put a gulf between man and God; it does not demean their user, does not cheat life of dignity, does not of itself desert men to the impersonal world of things. To use hammer, plane, chisel and saw belongs to a tradition which the Son of God himself reverenced. When he used the plumbline, the God-man lost none of his glory. The workshop is spiritually justifiable not simply as a Christian hobby for relaxation and pleasure; it is a legitimate area for week-long service of God and man. Indeed, the profound hope of the labor world in the twentieth century is the hammer and sickle in the hand of Christ and his servants and not in the grip of Karl Marx and the revolutionaries. Jesus Christ dignifies work by his personal example.

(4) *Early Christian believers maintained the dignity of work.* G. L. Treglown reminds us that the inscriptions and drawings in the catacombs discovered in Rome in 1578 depict believers in the course of daily work. The Greeks or Romans would hardly have perpetuated their image in the performance of such menial life tasks as farming, milking cows, and so on. Plato exalted the philosopher-king as the ideal guardian of the state, but the Christian movement was not embarrassed by the scarcity of philosophers in its ranks. Nor was it embarrassed because its first disciples included fishermen and a tax-gatherer, and because its greatest apostle was a tentmaker. Had not the Redeemer himself been a carpenter? First generation Christians reflected in daily living the biblically inspired conviction that manual work is noble.

3. Problems of the Contemporary Laborer

Many now maintain, however, that the Christian sense of vocation, once so powerful, is no longer relevant for the modern worker. Spurred by the industrial revolution and the machine age, far-reaching changes in the economic world have so altered the world of work — so it is contended — that the laboring man cannot respond to the Christian call.

Chief target of this criticism is the assembly line operation. Here the worker seems completely stripped of all creative significance. Depersonalized monotony seems to demote him to a subhuman cog in a gigantic machine. He suffers physically, mentally, and morally from detailed subdivision and standardization of labor. That this process raises the general standard of living by lessening production costs and bringing commodities within the purchasing power of lower income groups is hardly an adequate compensation for "debasing" the worker.

Unquestionably, the vast multiplication of non-creative jobs, the heightened routine and increase of mechanical operations, can play havoc with the creative aspirations of the individual. For this reason both Christian and non-Christian moralists have analyzed and criticized labor structures in the hope of preserving personal values. Already in 1831 Alexis de Tocqueville warned against degrading the workman. "What can be expected of a man," he said, "who has spent twenty years of his life in making heads for pins? and to what can that mighty human intelligence, which has so often stirred the world, be applied in him, except it be to investigate the best method of making pins' heads? When a workman has spent a considerable portion of his existence in this manner, his thoughts are forever set upon from the object of his daily toil; his body has contracted certain fixed habits which it can never shake off: in a word, he no longer belongs to himself, but to the calling which he has chosen."[10] In more recent times, not only Karl Marx but also critics inside the church have voiced similar criticism. Before the beginning of our century the Dutch theologian Abraham Kuyper complained that "to mistreat the workman as a 'piece of machinery' is and remains a violation of his human dignity. Even worse, it is a sin going squarely against the sixth commandment, thou shalt not kill, and this includes killing the worker socially."[11]

The Communist movement struck hard at the predicament of the worker in the machine age. To propagandize its thesis that capitalism degrades and exploits the laboring

[10] Alexis de Tocqueville, *Democracy in America* (New York: Knopf, 1948), II, 190.
[11] Abraham Kuyper, *Christianity and The Class Struggle* (Grand Rapids, Mich.: Piet Hein, 1950), p. 57.

class, and that Christian supernaturalism is irrelevant to the worker ("religion is the opiate of the masses"), Communism pointed not only to the universal enlistment of workers on the assembly line, but to special instances of shameful work conditions. Communists and socialists magnified such cases out of all proportion for the sake of anti-capitalist propaganda; their drive for labor reform gained much of its vitality from the shocking situations cited by the social revolutionists in their assault on free enterprise. In one factory, after several workers had lost their limbs in a press that required swift, hard operation, a device was finally invented which, hour after hour, automatically yanked the operator's hand and arm away from the descending press. That such situations should exist was a blow to the ethics of free enterprise and gave ammunition to the collectivisitic critique. These exceptional situations nourished the new naturalistic and collectivistic concepts of society and represented "this modern predicament of the worker" as a necessary consequence of free enterprise economics and of the social irrelevance of supernatural religion. Today the propaganda value of such exaggerations remains only where men are kept in ignorance and in political subjection to collectivistic rulers. Compared with those in Communist countries, working conditions and living standards now enjoyed by the laboring class in the Free World are known to be enviably high. In capitalistic countries the constant improvement of working conditions in this century has exposed the emptiness of collectivist contentions that intolerable exploitation is characteristic of capitalism, and necessary to its survival.

Surely Communism's betrayal of man's passion for freedom (in view of the subjection of individual rights to the totalitarian will of the state, and the consequent disregard of man's dignity and worth) ought to warn us against automatically accepting its criticism of the assembly line presumably out of concern for the worker's personal dignity. At least free enterprise is under no necessity to conform labor patterns to state dictatorship, and is free to revise assembly line techniques, should they be demonstrably injurious to the worker.

In fact, it is an evidence of Communism's moral shallowness that despite its long-standing negative propaganda, the Soviet sphere has imported and multiplied assembly lines, while it is the capitalist world that today wrestles earnestly with the problem. In projecting her own factories, Soviet Russia has hurried the pace of industrialization by dipping deeply into capitalistic techniques. For many years one Soviet factory in Gorky has produced more machine tools than the whole of Russia turned out in Czarist times. Through state planning and compulsion, the Soviet has become the world's second industrial power, showing a spectacular gain in steel production and other industrial basics. This swift advance, now ventured with considerably less success in Red China, depends on the adoption of the mass approach to work. The development of heavy machine industries, as well as the increased production of consumer goods, necessarily involves assembly line methods. With more than 45 million employed for some years in Russian trades industries, Pravda may editorialize about "mobilizing the creative energy of our people" for industrial development. But until the same indignation is shown behind the Iron Curtain as in non-Soviet lands over the "exploitation" of the worker on the assembly line, the world may well ascribe much of the collectivistic critique to propaganda rather than to morality. According to Communism, the capitalist structure requires laborers to earn their living as victims of big business. It should not be forgotten that by sowing its propaganda that "the state owes men a living," collectivism indirectly undermines the necessity of earning a living and instead encourages dependence upon the state for welfare and security. Actually, the failures of the welfare state have given fresh importance to the Christian virtue of work, which even at the elemental biological level of physical subsistence emphasizes the necessary labor of one's own hands (I Thess. 4:11f.; II Thess. 3:10).

Yet to expose the deceitfulness of Soviet propaganda, and even to emphasize the totalitarian subjection of the worker to the whim of the state, does not answer the basic problem. This fact is sure: multitudes of assembly line workers today *are* frustrated, and in the present conflict of world ideas they *are* encouraged to believe that capitalist structures are the direct cause of their distress. The seriousness of this situation cannot be overstated. Ian Henderson reminds us pointedly that "a society produces revolutionaries when it produces a frustrated class, a group who have no station and no duties in the society or one whose station in society allots to them only duties which give no scope for capabilities given them by God and developed by their own industry."[12]

How then, it is asked — granting that the assembly line is an element of technological civilization, and not a peculiarity of any one particular economic system — can individuality be protected, the sense of spirit and personal dignity be kept alive, in the whirl of mass production and assembly line techniques? Besides providing satisfactory work conditions and full concern for worker safety, what can industry do to relieve the drab routine that suppresses the sense of creativity and the thrill of work so significant in the Christian view of vocation? How, it is asked, can a person sit hour after hour in a factory, turning the same screw, or stapling the same box, and maintain the dignity of personality, the sense of creatively investing his talent to the glory of God?

If the assembly line necessarily degrades men into machines, and robs them of their destiny as sons of God in the world

---

[12] Ian Henderson, *Can Two Walk Together?* (London: Jas. Nisbet, 1948), p. 106.

of work, then Christianity has no alternative but to condemn the assembly line. Even the Old Testament, let alone the New, warns against ruling others "with rigor" (Lev. 25: 43), against oppressing the hired servant (Deut. 24:14), against "despising the cause" of manservant or maidservant (Job 31:13f.). If the assembly line destroys man's conviction of being a fellow-worker with God, if it dissolves his personal and spiritual well-being, then Christian social ethics must condemn it.

It must be said, however (although without condoning the assembly line (in all of its present patterns), that mental threat to spirituality and creativity of the worker is not posed by the assembly line. Actually, the machine age has been both boon and burden to the worker. At first it improved his lot, and relieved his daily drudgery; at the same time, by lessening hand labor, it also increased unemployment. Nor was it anticipated that endless division of labor might eventually deaden the human spirit and remove the feeling of spontaneity from the working scene. Sound absorbing equipment, on the one hand, and piped-in music, on the other, are now aimed to improve the worker's sense of well-being. But while his general spirit and efficiency have changed for the better, his feeling of the meaninglessness of his work remains the same. When his task follows the same routine hour after hour, week after week, even year after year, the worker's creative initiative and sense of personal worth seem to fade. While "rest periods" help to break the drab routine, they do not basically modify the day's monotony. While safety rules, shorter work weeks, more leisure time, and fringe benefits have improved the working atmosphere, and largely eliminated drab and uncongenial working conditions, the worker's inner spiritual unrest nonetheless often runs deeper than ever. Outward improvements and added material advantages may be a blessing for the worker, but they cannot guarantee his blessedness. Certain large manufacturers, like Ford Motor

58

Company and Westinghouse Electric, who periodically have changed the assembly line assignments of workers, have experienced no apparent loss of industrial efficiency, and have actually increased worker enthusiasm. It would appear, then, that there are creative techniques that both maintain worker efficiency and reduce the drab monotony of repetitious work. But human engineering may pose as much of a problem as job engineering. If job responsibilities are engineered to a point where little creativeness is necessary and human engineering is compounded with mechanical engineering, then the plight of the worker may be multiplied rather than relieved.

The Christian worker, however, even on the assembly line, can find a sense of ultimate purpose and meaning unknown to the unbeliever. While modern industry, at worst, may distort and thwart one's spiritual sonship during work hours, it cannot really make a machine of one who is a son of God. If one is truly a believer, no boss and no machine can pluck him out of Christ's hand and thrust him into a morass of meaninglessness. Even monotony can be justified in the ministry of God and of humanity, if it stems from a constructive activity that has no better alternative. Whatever contributes to the elevation and good of mankind is worthy, even if it lacks romance and novelty. The 340 permanent staff members of the Mayo Clinic are not less helpful to mankind because each individual is a specialist; repetition of the same task contributes not only to efficiency but to expertness. It is possible, of course, for vein specialists, or for those who bronchoscope patients all day long, to think of "pieces of humanity coming down the line." It is equally possible, and imperative, for the specialist with a sense of calling and mission to think of each person as "my private patient, to be handled as if he were the only patient I have." Someone will say that this high response is more natural to the worker who deals directly with the persons who benefit from his labors, and this is true enough. But no worker's responsibility is lessened simply because he serves an invisible neighbor. Many a life has been saved by a properly tightened screw, and many lost through an improperly tightened bolt.

The real drudgery of today's worker results not alone from his machine-bound existence on the assembly routine, but from a distaste for work itself. Because of his secularized misunderstanding, he dissociates the daily task from all mission either for God or man. Even the corporation executive complains that he is an "organization man," a mere cog in the wheel of business activity.

The problem, then, is not one merely of technological displacement; the basic difficulty is one of spiritual estrangement. The joylessness, the depressing drudgery of monotonous toil, are caused more by the worker than by the character of his work. "Demechanization" is too simple a solution for the unbeliever's problem; valid "personalizing" of work will come only with his own spiritual awakening.

When the American worker is compared with the vast majority of laborers elsewhere, it is apparent that almost all his lower level (survival and comfort) needs are now assured just by having been born in the United States. Yet these lower level satisfactions are the ones that labor organizations continually seek to widen, while they ignore higher level satisfactions that answer to the worker's inner needs. Only through spiritual commitment can higher satisfactions be restored to labor; only thus can the daily job, whatever its nature, be lifted above the continual danger of deteriorating into a wearisome monotony. No matter how challenging his job may appear, the worker who is estranged from the true religious significance of his task is often a spiritual pauper. The worker who abides in Christ, though he be a slave (the Apostle Paul spoke of a slavery quite different from that of the assembly line), can be the Lord's freeman (I Cor.

60

7:22). The Communist slander that capitalism makes slaves of workers can be met, therefore, not simply by showing that collectivist "freedom" is actually total enslavement to the state, nor simply by defending free enterprise economics, superior as this may be at the horizontal level, but by showing that man's inevitable enslavement through sin to tyrannical idols can be transcended only through slavery to Christ, who frees his servants as priests and kings.

Sometimes the routine of the assembly line permits more occasional conversation with one's fellow worker than does creative work. And the believer, always ready with a reason for his hope, will not be without something to say. The repetition of assembly line operation often gives opportunity for the Christian's friendly interest in his neighbor and for spiritual conversation. While the unbeliever is on the assembly line in bondage, the believer is free. But while the Christian is always ready with a word for his Lord, he must not allow spiritual conversation to encroach upon work priorities. He must beware of discrediting the Christian cause by neglecting his job in order to manifest spiritual concern.

As a disciple of Christ, the believer knows that if work is mere drudgery it is in the grip of sin. Work must be both a medium of service and a spiritual delight. On the other hand, not only the dullness of daily work but the thrill of it, the joy of its achievement, can constitute a spiritual hazard. Many Christians have short-changed themselves spiritually by being content with less than their fullest and best investment of God-given talent and skill. In fact, many a believer has been thwarted from a call to technical Christian service by his complacent gratification in other vocational activity. To turn a screw with Job-like patience on an assembly line is no reproach if it represents one's highest level of creative ability. Such limitation is sinful, however, for a disciple of Christ who has greater potential for service.

Sometimes the Protestant churches are reproached because they fail to reach the laboring masses — and it is regrettable that so many in the ranks of labor today are indeed outside the churches. This criticism overlooks the fact, however, that multitudes of believers, because of and in their spiritual commitment to Christ, have acquired new incentive and drive that lift them to new capacities and responsibilities. Christians called to technical divine service like the ministry or missions frequently testify that here, too, God provides the spiritual endowment and talent necessary to fulfill a special task. Mentioned among the New Testament gifts is that of "helps." If Protestantism is sometimes caricatured as "the religion of the middle classes," it must not be forgotten how many have been lifted to new incentive and achievement through the power of regenerative religion.

In the contemporary situation, the Christian doctrine of vocation is sometimes dismissed as irrelevant not only because of the assembly line, but also because of restrictions imposed on the working man by big business and organized labor. These restrictions are often of such a nature, it is held, that the worker is no longer significantly free to exercise his volition on the daily job. The demands of management for increased production, or the adoption of a "go slow" policy by a union, represent a quantitative approach to work that destroys craftsmanship and may involve the worker in selfish and unethical situations as the price of his job. Unions sometimes adopt a "go slow" policy to circumvent management's automatic expectation of greater production, or to avoid overproduction that threatens unemployment, or to deprive shareholders of greater profits. Thus the work schedule is dictated not by worker ability but by promised reward for the organization man and by fear of retribution for the uncooperative.

Featherbedding, or loafing on the job, has become an acute problem. The worker holds his job not to earn what he gets, but primarily to collect what he gets for so many hours. This practice is so widespread that in the case of some railroads, for example, any margin between profit and loss is virtually erased by union work rules that encourage featherbedding. This issue was also at stake in the steel strike of 1959-60 and the threatened railroad strike of 1962-63. An outstanding AFL-CIO labor leader, Andrew Harvey, acknowledged that "if all workers put forth their best efforts in construction, today's new homes would cost up to 25 per cent less per unit." Both worker and employer should have a voice in determining work rules. But they ought also to stipulate *moral* rules for fulfilling work and not loopholes for evading it. Alongside "the workman is worthy of his hire" belongs "if any would not work, neither should he eat" (II Thess. 3:10). It becomes the responsibility of labor leaders, therefore, not only to protect the job security of their forces, but also to protect the right of management to expect an honest day's work. Even union-management agreements to reduce featherbedding in construction work have failed to eliminate so-called "make work" practices. Unions stipulate the top limits of a member's daily work production; in turn, to escape the consequent inflated labor costs, the management of heavy construction companies welcomes technological improvements that permit greater production at less expense. Unions sometimes give only lip service to agreements in respect to "slowdowns, forcing of overtime, spread-work tactics, stand-by crews and featherbedding practices. . . ." Some unions have demanded a minimum of three days' pay for jobs that require only a half day's work. The main concern, obviously, is not over the coffee break or siesta time, but rather over a lack of sustained job performance for which the worker expects full pay and all the fringe benefits. In depression days, the Works Project Administration called such practice "boondoggling"; the military dubs it "goldbricking" or just "goofing off." Besides such "go slow" policies during union contract periods, unions may use their power to boycott firms (such as the Kohler Company) if strike and picket line negotiations have failed, and thus snare the hapless worker for destructive purposes. That is, the union will deliberately ruin a company if it refuses to come to union terms which have already been rejected as neither reasonable nor just.

Since Christianity exalts not self-centeredness but Christ-centeredness, how can the committed worker submit to selfish demands either of management or labor without lowering his ideals? This problem is not hypothetical but extremely acute for the Christian worker. While Scripture admonishes him to respect authority even in his labors (I Tim. 6:1; Tit. 2:9; I Pet. 2:18), yet first and foremost the Christian worker is to please God as his supreme master (Eph. 6:5-7; Tit. 2:10; I Pet. 2:19). This tension exists in many organizations, and here and there has led to formation of chapters of the Christian Labor Association, a union organized professedly on Christian principles which promises the worker an opportunity to carry the spirit of prayer to the factory and office.

"Union with Christ," of course, supplies that rarified climate where both management and labor can best resolve their differences. At the very least, Christian workers and Christian management, too, can acknowledge what partnership with God means in word and on the job. Christian management involves more than a profession of faith by the head of the firm, more than liberal investment of his profits in missionary or church enterprises and of his time in preaching the Gospel. Christian management means also that in the world of work the executive translates into employer-employee relationships what it means to dedicate business to the glory of God in the service of man. When Christian employers refuse to conform their organizations to the established, sometimes corrupt, patterns of the secular economic world, they have an opportunity to shape higher and exemplary types of employer-employee relationships and activities. To make Christ the master of both the Christian worker and employer, to place both under his command as "the Boss," certainly does not dissolve the authority of management, but it does exclude both the cringing worker and the tyrannical employer. The industrial chaplaincy program practiced by many organizations has much to commend it. If it concentrates only on personal decisions, however, or, on the other hand, substitutes for the Gospel only a program of ethical idealism or moralism, then it does not really offer a spiritual reinterpretation of work. When God takes charge, production speeds which exhaust a worker in a decade, or routines which reduce him to a mere mechanical cog, come to an end; to be in God's employ brings pride in one's work and a contagious sense of creative contribution and service. Such an atmosphere gives the Christian worker a unique opportunity (seldom granted to his minister) of being a spokesman for God among his colleagues and of lifting them beyond the tensions of greed to the level of God's justice and grace.

Most workers today, however, are in "religiously neutral" unions where the ideal of "service," let alone of "the service of God," is missing. But even here the Christian need not feel "alone" in his efforts for righteousness. He can be a "union" man without upholding every organized cause, for he belongs first of all to the greatest union of workers, the body of Christ, of which the Lord himself is the infallible and exalted head. The Christian need not be anti-union, for the Christian message is, after all, one of reconciliation. Whenever the union is anti-God, however, the Christian has no choice: he must be anti-union. Nor is the worker expected to be blindly pro-management; even as his primary union is the body of Christ, so God is the believer's main "boss." The wide publicity given to union strikes, such as that aimed in the past at the steel and railroad industries, tends to exaggerate the tensions between labor and management. Fortunately, many firms today rest on a deeper interior loyalty than that acknowledged in "class" propaganda; in the final analysis, management and labor are convinced they share mutual interests and a solid corporate spirit. But in times of economic stress, or of organizational pressures, even such a bond is insufficient to preserve the mutuality of management and labor, and when spiritual controls are absent, economic issues may easily provoke resentment and rivalry. In recent years profit-sharing or ownership-sharing plans have gained in popularity. Such programs draw management and labor closer together by providing the worker with additional compensation for his work. But, it should be noted, while they enlarge the sharing of management's profits, they do not proportionately share its risks and losses.

The Pauline doctrine of vocation has at times been discredited by those who misapplied "let every man abide in the same calling wherein he was called" (I Cor. 7:20) in order to stifle social unrest, and to bypass economic and social inequities. Calvin, however, stressed that it was wrong to consider one's place in the social order as necessarily static and fixed. He found in this Scripture passage not a call for believers to continue in the kind of life they had begun, which required the lower orders of society to remain content with their present work indefinitely, but rather a caution against restlessness.

Certainly John the Baptist's exhortation "be content with your wages" needs to be coupled with "the worker is worthy of his hire" (Luke 10:7). These two New Testament passages simply mean that service is the ultimate approach to vocation from the Christian perspective. Yet the first passage implies, too, a caution against impermanence in one's work. The present turnover of employees from one place of employment to another, primarily for higher wages or greater marginal benefits, is no secret. Those who flit from one job to another in search of maximal economic returns often remain unskilled and jeopardize the satisfying use of their talents for the good of the cultural enterprise. Progressive development and use of such talents could in time also have afforded an adequate living. In other words, transient workers contribute not only to economic instability but also to the deterioration of spiritual satisfaction that comes from maximum achievement. Many persons, even Christian, are motivated more by restlessness than by conviction to change the location or nature of their work. In fact, vocational vagabondage may cast doubt upon one's claim to be working in the place of God's assignment, for it is quite proper for the Christian to speak of his "chosen life work." The economic pursuit, after all, requires one of life's most far-reaching decisions. Paul's exhortation to "abide in one's station" therefore has genuine relevance for the modern spirit of vocational upheaval. The laborer who comes into spiritual commitment to Christ while on a particular job has no reason on that ground to desert his job, if it be respectable, and to cast about at once for something different. God calls the believer to serve in many different honest and legitimate occupations, even though such assignments at times may seen uninteresting and confining.

The sense of divine vocation in a given job does not coincide necessarily with the work preferences of the regenerate man, nor with those of parents for their children. In each generation God seeks to release the full potential of each of his followers. Personal assessment of one's special gifts, vocational aptitude tests, the discerning counsel of others, and community needs are all helpful for making vocational choices. The community's well-being is a legitimate contemplation; surely it is better for a believer — if these are the options — to be a garbage collector than a liquor salesman. The continuing and not merely present demand for workers like teachers, doctors, scientists, contractors, and so on, is another determining factor in vocational choice. And by their very training, college students have a wider range of choices for their life work.

But the Christian's avenue of service is not determined primarily by the question of where he can "do the most good," any more than where he stands "to get the most out of it." The basic determinant, rather, is "where God wants me." What to the man of the world is a "career," is to the Christian a "calling." Unfortunately, state welfare policies, attentive to the worker's wants as much as his needs, often assure him more financial security in the way of favorable hours, attractive wages, substantial pensions, unemployment insurance and other benefits, than the voluntary agencies do, let alone can. In our money-minded times, moreover, financial success often comes most swiftly not on the basis of talent and industry, but because of patronage or of willingness to sacrifice integrity or decency for the sake of gain. Our generation is not the first, however, when Christians have had to protest the notion that material affluence is what determines the abundant life. Samuel Zwemer said that from a human point of view the years he spent among the Moslems of Africa might seem a failure. But even where true failure does come, God gives other opportunities, as both Jonah and John Mark experienced. Sustained prayer, therefore, is as appropriate and indispensable in deciding about vocation as it is in deciding about marriage.

The Bible gives no detailed instruction concerning avenues of work, not because it deals with primitive societies but because this aspect of life is a matter of spiritual decision in which the Lord also makes known his way (Matt. 28:20; Rom. 8:28). Seldom does he disclose to believers their whole biography in advance; step by step he "leads his dear chil-

dren" to entrust marriage, health, and all else to his provi-
dences. Not simply in the larger society and in the world,
but already in the intimacy of the family and home is the
distinction of callings evident. Heredity and environment
allow less vocational range for some Christians than for
others. All are obligated to do their best, however, and no
one who can justify his labors as the service of God and
man is to be disparaged as ordinary. Collegians may be
called to major in philosophy, but they are seldom called
in college to be philosophers; seminarians may be called to
specialize in theology, but they are usually not called to be
professional theologians at the level of bachelor of divinity
studies. But one *present* calling of the student is sure, even
if his future calling is in doubt: every young person registered
in a Christian college or university is called to be a *student*.

Not all Christians are technically superior, by any means.
Even those who are, ought not to be "pushed" into the
ministry on that account. The clergyman has neither the
duty nor the right to press the layman to leave his secular
work for ordination to the preaching ministry, just as the
layman has no duty or right to urge the clergyman to leave
his vocation "to serve tables." Furthermore, the *place* of
service is as important as the kind. As Hogben has said, a
dislocated member becomes a source of pain and embarrass-
ment to the body, not a help and strength. Christian strategy
in a pagan world makes this factor of location important;
the geographical placement of an army may be more decisive in battle than its numerical strength.

Let the Christian also take care how he uses his *tongue*
on the job. That he will not profane the name of Christ,
nor resort to profanity at all, is almost too elemental to
suggest. How much or how little should he say by way
of Christian witness? Even the pagan who never mentions
the name of Christ at least avoids its use in profanity thereby! As already noted, the assembly line provides some

latitude for spiritual conversation with one's neighbor, and the Christian — instead of avoiding the topic of religion (which barbers and others classify as off-limits with patrons) — will not hesitate to bring spiritual realities into normal conversation. The "office grapevine" has an effect on morale, workmanship and co-operation; in one way or another the Christian worker has opportunity to use it for good. But what are the proper limits of spiritual conversation on the job? Certainly they are defined in part by the response of the listener (the Christian worker, too, as an alert listener understands how to turn even complaints into points of contact with the soul. Even industry has channeled the gripe into the suggestion box. In 1953, 4000 companies got two million ideas, adopted one in five, and paid $15 million in awards).

But a full sense of work responsibility is vital too. The Christian has no license to squander time for which he is paid to work. Nor can spiritual talk be an excuse for shoddy craftsmanship. A significant part of a Christian worker's witness is the quality of his work as well as the attitude toward his work. To say "I'm a soul-winner, but I cobble shoes to pay expenses" is both right and wrong: while Christian witness is always a believer's responsibility, the work he does involves far more than a means of livelihood and carries tremendous spiritual overtones. That he make good cabinets and shelves is the very first demand that his religion makes upon the Christian carpenter as a worker.

A photographer who takes poor pictures, even though he is an effective soul-winner, should either take his vocation more seriously, change his business, or at least confine his witness to non-customers! No impressive list of converts will offset a poor work record; one's work ought not to be of such questionable calibre that it disgraces God, discredits one's employer, and affronts society. What distinguishes the Christian worker from the unbeliever is the sense of mission

70

he demonstrates in his labors. The housewife who placed this sign over the kitchen sink had the right idea of her particular calling: "Divine service held here three times daily." The message of Christ's Lordship to the worker is simply this: "God wants *you* . . . in *your job*."

III. THE CHRISTIAN STAKE IN LEGISLATION: THEORETICAL CONSIDERATIONS

ALTHOUGH THE CHRISTIAN CHURCH OUGHT TO RELY ON THE spiritual regeneration of individuals to *transform* society, it must not on that account neglect the role of education and legislation in *preserving* what is valuable in the present social order. Christian social theory needs to distinguish between transforming and preserving, and to recognize that education and legislation can serve only the latter of these ends. But preserving the good in society is worth doing, and the Church dare not yield total control of education and legislation to secular agencies.

In this first of two chapters on the theme of "The Christian Stake in Legislation" we shall mainly consider theoretical aspects of the subject, deferring the treatment of practical problems to the subsequent chapter.

1. SOME HISTORICAL FACTORS

The apostolic truth that the company of the redeemed constitutes a new society all too soon gave way to the larger ecclesiastical ambition to Christianize the outside world. In John T. McNeill's words, "The exalted sense of mission to save souls from a doomed world into a heavenly commonwealth began to be modified by the conception of a saving or preserving function to be exercised by the church as a universal leaven in an improvable world."[1] McNeill locates

[1] J. T. McNeill, *Christian Hope for World Society* (Chicago: Willett & Clark, 1937), p. 3.

the first intimations of this new concept in the first half of the second century. Thereafter the notion that the Christian religion bears divine responsibility for holding together all the social frontiers of human existence, and is obliged therefore to shape a new world, became a main motif of Catholic Christendom. The consequent medieval union of Church and State was not transcended until Calvin objectified the State as distinct from the Church and assigned positive individual functions to each.

Scattered as they are throughout all the nations of the world, Christians more than ever before live under a great variety of governments as a result of the political upheavals of our generation. Their opportunities and methods of political action differ widely, as do their relationships to legislative processes. Someone like myself, who believes that the representative form of government has much to commend it, even that it incorporates political virtues and blessings to an exceptional degree, must nonetheless guard against over-adulating or uncritically supporting some particular form of government. Nor can he require Christians living under quite different forms of political order to follow patterns of duty that are possible only on the American scene.

From British history we learn that theological as well as political patterns underlie many of the divergent ecclesiastical approaches. By coupling rejection of the Pope's external authority in political affairs with a determination to preserve Christian polity on a national basis, England and Scotland retained major elements of medieval tradition. They emphasized national religion and a national testimony to its truth. This involved, among other things, a Christian polity (scriptural instead of papal) in public affairs and led, in time, to the idea of a constitution for a Christian state. Although championed as a Presbyterian theocracy whose inspiration, foundation and textbook was the Bible, the Scottish state derived its polity largely from Old Testament teaching for

73

the Hebrew state, and viewed legislation mainly as an external code for regulating society. In England the idea of a Christian realm did not involve a theocracy; it did, however, involve national Christianity and a national church, blending religious and secular interests to promote at one and the same time the spiritual, political, and economic good of the community. Over against this view William Cunningham, in his instructive Lowell Lectures, traces the protest of the Independents. They "altogether rejected any system of National Christianity," and stressed "personal conviction as the basis of all true Church life. Instead of putting Christian society in the forefront and thinking of the individual character as formed and moulded by this environment, they regarded the individuals as the constituent elements who associated themselves into a religious society."[2] Emphasis on the Christian duty of the secular community thus gave way to emphasis on the public duty of the Christian community, or rather, the community responsibility of Christians as individuals. The Quakers went still further, and assailed the actual content of national Christianity. Recognizing only individual conscience and personal morality as absolute, they rejected war and oaths. Quakers insisted that the motivation for a believer's duty, whether in public or private life, remains always the same; they criticized what passed for Christian conduct in public affairs and rejected any concept of political morality or Christian polity not expressly based on the Sermon on the Mount. The next move toward isolationism came from dissident sectarian groups who viewed all established civil order as profane. Christian principles are inapplicable to it, they contended; Christians should withdraw from it entirely, therefore, in order to realize the will of God exclusively in a spiritual fellowship of believers.

Even today, debate over the Christian philosophy of the

---

[2] W. Cunningham, *Christianity and Politics* (Boston: Houghton Mifflin, 1915), p. 92.

State occurs on almost all the frontiers of twentieth century Christendom, and is not confined to American liberals and evangelicals. Lutheran and Reformed churchmen abroad are reassessing the nature and work of the State, in the light not only of confessional differences but also of novel views expounded by contemporary theologians.[3] The broken impact of Christian ideals on Western political life vexes the religious community on almost every national front. In the past no force influenced the course of Western politics for good or ill more than religion; even the American understanding of Church-State separation emerged from religious considerations rather than from secular political theory. Now the problem is inverted. Skepticism has overtaken both the concepts of a national religion and of a Christian polity, and there is mounting doubt about the political relevance of the religion that survives in national life. Some awareness of national destiny may survive, and even some feeling of national duty toward other nations, but there is no longer a full sense of political mission to the world. How then preserve a significant role for religion in politics, which has divorced itself from religious priorities both in principle and in practice? This problem is not confined to totalitarian lands hostile to religion; it is equally acute in lands where state religion has lost its popular grip, and in democratic societies unaware that high political dedication must be sustained voluntarily by spiritual motivations. The religious tolerance boasted by the Western nations in our time more and more betrays itself, when analyzed, as a blithe indifference to religion. The feeling is extant that any and every introduction of religious claims will only confuse the national climate and disturb the direction of political life.

That the problem of politics for twentieth century Christianity is of major importance cannot be gainsaid. George W. Forell thinks this problem just as crucial in our century

[3] Cf. Adolf Keller, *Church and State on the European Continent* (London: Epworth Press, 1936), pp. 344ff.

as was that of faith in the sixteenth or the problem of truth in the eighteenth century.[4] Nothing has so much revived the conviction that Christianity must somehow become a force in political life as has the irreligious spirit of the modern totalitarian trend. This trend, by challenging the political significance of the individual, contravenes a spirit that was fostered in the West by the Greek democratic tradition, was reinforced by the new middle class in Anglo-Saxon life, was extended by the French and American revolutions, and was sanctified by Protestant Christian concepts of individual responsibility. Whatever we may think about the fact, political forces are indeed determining the future more and more. And while the Christian movement needs to challenge the dogma that political means will solve all the problems of mankind, it may not neglect to use these means for the achieving of proper and legitimate objectives. The Church must expound the revealed will of God for the political order no less than for the other spheres of life, for all are answerable and subject to divine judgment.

Protestantism is in fact divided over the bearing of Christian faith on political questions. Forell's distinction between three contemporary approaches to this situation is noteworthy, even though he over-restricts the dimensions of the problem. There are those, he comments, who consider Christianity wholly irrelevant to politics. Second, there are those who apply its relevance only to secondary concerns of personal piety. A third group, says Forell, simply associates Christianity with the political *status quo*.[5] While these approaches are indeed conspicuous, a fourth position has gained disturbing prominence, namely, that the Christian Church as an institution may and should lend its moral prestige to particular, detailed politico-economic measures by official endorsement. Ameri-

4 G. W. Forell, "Law and Gospel as a Problem of Politics," in *Religion in Life* (Summer, 1962).
5 *Ibid.*

can Protestantism is presently debating whether the Church plays an appropriate part in shaping new politico-economic frontiers, or whether she betrays her mandate by "meddling in politics." What is proper and improper for the Church in the arena of political thought and activity? Specially needful today is an exposition that maintains relevance for the political scene by suggesting a desirable course of action for American Protestantism.

2. THE CHURCH AND SOCIAL LEGISLATION

The phenomena of church government, canon law, and ecclesiastical discipline of moral evil attest the Church's undeniable interest in law and government. These practices, of course, are not aspects of civil government and statute law. But they inevitably confront the Church with the question of the ideal relationship between the Divine Lawgiver and Divine government on one hand and human laws and civil government on the other. It is true, of course, that divine and human elements are incorporated into both church and civil government, but the connection between the will of God and human duty is necessarily raised in connection with ecclesiastical morality. A fundamental analysis of politics from a Christian point of view lies outside the scope of this study, but it remains one of the urgent tasks of our age.

While among its own constituency the Church may legislate its moral code under threat of discipline, it is not free to force its distinctive requirements upon society as a whole through techniques of pressure and compulsion. When the Roman Catholic Church in the later Middle Ages, the so-called "golden age of the canonists," sought to enforce its code upon "the still half-heathen kingdoms of the world," it was as much wrong as when earlier Christian ideas were stamped upon the barbarians through a "Christianized Roman law." The Roman Church's tendency to exercise external spiritual authority over political life wherever possible, and to subject

77

nations to its own religious claims, has achieved little in the way of political and social progress. There is little evidence that the lands benefited by the Protestant Reformation are eager to return to Papal guidance in affairs of state. Wherever ecclesiastical hierarchies have sought to conform secular law to church law, thereby extending the authority of church law to encompass virtually all of life, Christianity has lost ground in the long run. Under ecclesiastical influence politicians have sometimes adopted proposals initiated and promoted by the Church, so that the Church was not openly responsible for their enforcement. The end-results have been the same, however: ecclesiastical exploitation of the State, and political deterioration of religion. In the Middle Ages "Popes could engage in warfare for purely temporal ends; bishops and monasteries used their influence to amass wealth."[6] To impose a particular theory of society and Christian moral ideals upon unresponsive masses both abuses ecclesiastical influence and breeds resentment of church interference in government. Even apart from trying to impose a comprehensive Christian program on society, the Church breeds reaction whenever it seeks to enforce certain precepts that are unsupported by public opinion. At one time swearing was fined in England, and adultery punished by death.

The Church as *Church* is not to seek from government its own favored prestige and power in the political realm, nor to support merely what contributes to its own advancement. Says Karl Barth, "In the political sphere the Church will not be fighting for itself and its own concerns. Its own position, influence and power in the State are not the goal which will determine the trend of its political decisions. ('My Kingdom is not of this world . . . .' John 18:36). The secret contempt which a Church fighting for its own interests with

6 S. L. Greenslade, *The Church and the Social Order* (London: SCM Press, 1948) p. 75.

3. THEORETICAL CONSIDERATIONS

political weapons usually incurs even when it achieves a certain amount of success, is well deserved . . . ."[7]

To achieve a Christian society by political action is, therefore, not the Church's objective. Using government as a transforming agency to produce a social utopia, and projecting the Kingdom of God as essentially politico-economic in character, have harmed both the character of pure religion and the cause of government. In such attempts, the Christian religion neglects its distinctive message and its distinctive dynamism for social regeneration, and the state loses its proper passion for justice in sentimental theories of benevolence that simply tend to substitute the special privileges of one class or group for those of another.

Through government of its own members, the Church indirectly promotes the welfare of society as a whole. Its moral demands obviously overlap broad aspects of general social conduct, especially in sexual and marital concerns. Since the family is fundamental to society, the Church's administration of marriage vows — even if it is not free to demand a religious ceremony — gains importance by upholding the ideal of unbroken union and mutual obligation of one man and one woman. When the Church requires her membership to practice Christian principles in everyday life it unavoidably touches upon many areas of conduct subject also to civil legislation.

3. THE OBSERVANCE OF CIVIC LAW

The devout man must respect law, and he is spiritually inclined to obey the positive law of the State. But the Christian's duty involves not simply the observance of those statutes which seem to strengthen the Decalogue. Nor is it the Christian view to condition one's support of the State upon its promotion of Christian religious principles, and to withhold support

---

[7] K. Barth, *Against the Stream* (New York: Philosophical Library, 1954), pp. 29f.

unless the State operates on explicitly sectarian principles. We have already emphasized that the political order does not exist for the enforcement of sectarian objectives.

Ancient Roman justice was often brutal in method and corrupt in administration. Yet the New Testament repeatedly emphasizes the positive role even of that pagan state and stresses the importance of constructive citizenship on this broad basis. "The author of Acts is eager to show that St. Paul, the servant of the gospel, was also a loyal and dutiful citizen of the Roman Empire, and that Roman magistrates and governors recognized him to be such, whenever they were not misled by accident or slander," says O. C. Quick, in asking us to "consider the part played by Roman law and justice in assisting the spread of the gospel and safeguarding the nascent life of the Christian Church. . . . If it had not on the whole protected the rights and liberties of its subjects against the zeal of a persecuting religion," he continues, "Jewish bigotry would have made short work of St. Paul's mission to the Gentiles. And St. Paul was well aware of the debt which Christianity owed to Roman justice. To him its sword was that which restrained the lawless one, and so allowed scope to the gospel to do its work beyond law."[8] The distinction between good and evil exists even for and in the heathen State. The Christian must not withhold active support from the State, therefore, because of its heathen (or non-Christian) nature, but only if and when the State makes excessive or totalitarian demands.

The Christian's duty to support the State includes observance of tax laws and laws of community order such as speed limits, parking regulations, and so on. He is not to begrudge such obedience to statute law, as if the demands of civil government represent an unavoidable encroachment upon Christian liberty. The Christian community must promote public morality by

[8] O. C. Quick, *Christianity and Justice* (London: Sheldon Press, 1940), pp. 50ff.

personal example and a positive spirit toward the State. This requirement is implicit in various scriptural injunctions.

4. SPECIFIC DUTIES TO GOVERNMENT

Believers are to pray for rulers (not against them), and, as Jesus exhorted, they are to "render unto Caesar" what is ideally Caesar's; Paul declares that the powers rule by divine ordination and authority. "It is true," Barth notes, "that the deepest, ultimate divine purpose of the civil community consists in creating opportunities for the preaching and hearing of the Word and, to that extent, for the existence of the Church. But the only way the State can create such opportunities, according to the providence and ordinance of God, is the natural, secular and profane way of the establishment of law, the safeguarding of freedom and peace. . . ."[9] The Church respects an eternal justice and an authoritative law which is transcendent and objective, and which, on the ground that all men are responsible creatures answerable to their Creator, allows and preserves the rights of non-Christians as well as of Christians.

The Church is obliged not simply to pray in private, but also, as part of the whole counsel of God, to proclaim publicly the divinely intended role of civil government. But this proclamation involves more than preaching political duty and morality to its own members (even when religious indifference and widespread dislike of the Church's moral standards might encourage this restriction). The Church must lead men to understand government as a guardian of justice, must condemn legal infractions as crimes against the State, and must emphasize the culpability of offenders and their need to repent.

But the Church must not stop even here. It has the right and duty to call upon rulers, even pagan rulers, to maintain order and justice. It must stress the divine responsibility of

[9] Barth, *op. cit.*, p. 30.

government, condemn every repudiation of divine answerability, and challenge the State's neglect of its duty. The Church cannot content itself simply with denying church membership to the unjust and politically immoral. It must also criticize those who violate, misapply, or refuse to enforce the law. In Barth's words, the Church is to call the State "into co-responsibility before God."[10]

5. THE NEED FOR CHRISTIAN GUIDELINES

Even though the Church is not arbitrarily to impose a theology of society, forcing its ideals upon the world, it needs to do more than merely criticize the political climate, no matter how justifiable and effective such censure may sometimes be. Is there really any excuse for not suggesting constructive alternatives to the unpromising attempts to gain political order in an atmosphere of spiritual indifference?

We may indicate five reasons why the Church ought to address rulers and the populace on the theme of proper social principles.

(1) If the Church fails to apply the central truths of the Christian religion to social problems correctly, someone else will do so *incorrectly*. Much of the strength of socialistic theories, even if they are actually anti-theological when assessed from a biblical point of view, has been gained from the fact that some socialist thinkers have offered a supposedly Christian sociology. However misguided, the "Christian Socialists" in England, for example, professed to work out the social implications of Christian theology — a society built on the presuppositions of divine creation, incarnation, and redemption. Because socio-political obligations devolve inescapably upon all Christians as citizens of two worlds, the Church is obliged to indicate what it means for political theory that the Christian life is to be maintained not only distinct from the world, but in relevant and responsible rela-

10 *Ibid.,* p. 34.

tionship to the whole social-cultural realm, and to demonstrate the proper performance of political duty.

(2) At the very least, the Church should address government in order to dispel misunderstanding of its attitudes toward the State, if not also for the sake of self-protection and self-preservation (ultimately, the Lord is the Protector and Preserver of the Church). What made it legally possible in Christ's day for the Roman politicians to crucify Jesus on the trumped-up charge that he was a zealot? For one thing, it was Pilate's lack of interest in establishing Jesus' real attitude toward the State. Beyond that, the false expectation even of Jesus' disciples that the Messianic promise would be fulfilled by sudden political revolution may also have encouraged misunderstanding of their Messiah's intentions. Today the wrong understanding of the Christian view of the State is compounded both by the Roman Catholic theory of union of Church and State and the Protestant liberal attempt to spawn the Kingdom of God as an earthly politico-economic development. Neither scheme has escaped the notice of totalitarian rulers who want to manipulate the Church for their own political objectives. Other ecclesiastical movements, on the other hand, have withdrawn almost entirely from the political arena, only to be suspected of enmity toward the State, if not of anarchistic views that in principle renounce the State's validity entirely. "Many a persecution of Christians could have been avoided," Oscar Cullmann thinks, "if the State had taken pains to *understand* their attitude and convince itself of their loyalty. The cross of Christ in itself should remind all responsible statesmen to examine the Christian's real attitude toward the State."[11] Cullmann appropriately notes, moreover, that in I Peter Christians are reminded "to instruct the State concerning the true attitude of Christians."[12]

[11] O. Cullmann, *The State in the New Testament* (New York: Chas. Scribner's Sons, 1956), p. 55.
[12] *Ibid.*, p. 55, n.i. Cf. John Knox, "Pliny and I Peter: A Note on I Peter 4:14-16 and 3:15," *Journal of Biblical Literature* (1955), pp. 187ff.

(3) In view of the many modern totalitarian views that idolatrize the State as the lord of all life, the biblical exposition of the legitimate but limited authority of civil government gains special urgency. Recent secular interpretations of government lend additional importance to the Church's legitimate role, if not as a spiritual watchman over the State, at least as a moral sentry within it. By courageous preaching the Church must identify as inimical to God any excessive demands of the State in the religio-ideological realm, and refuse to render to Caesar what is not his due.

When the State assumes, as V. A. Demant puts it, "that there is no law of justice, no spiritual standards, no scientific truth, but only such as are 'good' in the sense of ministering to the power of the omnicompetent State,"[13] then the Church must unhesitatingly affirm that the State speaks beyond its competence and surpasses its proper sovereignty. Satan entrenches himself in false centers of authority, and the Church in its battle against evil dare not view political powers with indifference and outside its sphere of conflict. "The demonic is the lust for power in all its forms and patterns, power for power's sake without any ethical norms, the will to power beyond the limits set by God, power without law," writes Eivind Berggrav, the Lutheran bishop imprisoned by the Nazis after their invasion of Norway. "Everything in us is satanic which wants to dominate and is not willing to . . . serve God. . . . When the state insists on being totalitarian, e.g., when it considers itself a philosophy of life and insists on forcing this view on others, then . . . the devil is on the loose."[14] Berggrav reminds us that the real alternatives in the political realm are "whether the state is going to be a power which seeks to dominate the entire life of its citizens (perchance under the guise

13 V. A. Demant, "The Problems of Church and State," in *Christian Polity* (London: Faber and Faber, 1936), p. 129.
14 E. Berggrav, *Man and State* (Philadelphia: Muhlenberg Press, 1951), p. 305.

of democratic forms) or an instrument through which citizens may work together for the common weal."[15]

The Christian view of the function of government in human life alerts men against State regimentation of personal affairs, and guards against government displacement of individual responsibility. Had it been relevantly presented in its true light and vigor, the Christian theory of government would have challenged the recent modern glorification of the State in Germany, in Russia, and throughout the Soviet sphere. It would also have retarded the exaltation of the community and the consequent collectivization which even in so-called democratic nations has approached a social revolution.

Professor Quick observes how anti-religious totalitarian powers today exceed the moral delinquency of the pagan Roman Empire which vexed and persecuted so many of the early Christians. "The totalitarian State, whatever its colour, acknowledges no principle of common and impartial 'fairness,' which binds everyone and every part, both government and subject, alike. In spite of all its faults of cruelty and oppression, and in spite even of the iniquitous institution of slavery, the heathen government of Rome did dimly and uncertainly acknowledge such a principle; and therefore on the whole its law protected the infant Church even to the undoing of its own heathenism. But the party-governments of totalitarian States today cannot conceive of any justice which is not partisan. . . . The contrast shows . . . how dependent the propagation of the gospel may be on the forcible maintenance of a justice which in itself has no quality of love at all."[16] In the light of world political conditions, the duty of teaching the law of righteousness as well as of proclaiming the Gospel of redemption now devolves upon the Church more urgently than ever before.

The Church ought to avoid, rather than to seek, a truce

---

[15] *Ibid.*, p. 3.
[16] Quick, *op. cit.*, pp. 51f.

whereby, on condition of support of a particular government, Christians are allowed to pursue sectarian objectives. The danger is as great when Protestants in Nicaragua stand ready to support whatever government allows evangelicals to exert their influence as when Roman Catholics act on a similar thesis in Spain. The Church must be ever ready to warn against any transgressions by the State of its proper limits; it ought to seek religious freedom, not sectarian favors. In Norway the churches by collective action were able to do something to keep from being "ground under," as were the churches of Germany by Hitler. The Church's "self-interest" in matters of government is found in the protection of the rights of all.

(4) Assertion of the Christian view of government is imperative not only because of totalitarian trends but also because political democracy today often survives in a climate of relativism in socio-political affairs. Where it is no longer held that the individual is somehow directly related to the eternal, it is scarcely possible to maintain that the State must secure the rights of the individual. "It is the new and radical disbelief in eternity, so characteristic of the modern world," Quick tells us, "which is the real cause of a new and radical totalitarianism."[17] The notion that "Christian morality is personal and social and in its nature cannot be political," expressed in the forepart of our generation by writers like F. von Bernhardi[18] has led to the concept that the State is a law unto itself, and in times of crisis the only conscience of its citizens. The fruit of such theory is a government not only barren of Christian principles, but wholly devoid of Christian restraints. Increasingly the moral chaos of our times rationalizes democratic forms of government in terms of sheer trial and error. Carl J. Friedrich's words reflect this very mood: "Whether there be an ultimate right or wrong,

17 *Ibid.*, p. 7.
18 F. von Bernhardi, *Germany and the Next War* (New York: Longmans, Green & Col., 1914; London: E. Arnold, 1914) , p. 29.

good or bad, no man knows what it is. In the absence of such absolute standards, communal policies depend upon calculations of probability."[19] Is not this ethical confusion and ignorance of transcendent principles a "Macedonian call" for the Church to address the political order? The need is all the more imperative because, as Edward L. Long, Jr., remarks, so few people "recognize the contrast between the secularized standards of our age and the moral principles of Christianity"; instead, the multitudes "harbor the vague illusion that our common life is 'Christian'."[20]

To lose transcendent criteria, and a fixed and objective morality, can only end in subjectivism, and perpetuate the whole present morass of misunderstanding in ethics. And, as Berggrav warns, the road from relativism to arbitrary totalitarianism is much shorter than we are prone to think. "The society which promotes the maximum amount of spontaneous authority (truth and justice) in the souls of its people will be best equipped to resist demonism. . . . Unless the state sets things in order for those forces which can give authority-producing centers to the life of its people, then the state will soon succumb to the forces of evil."[21] Representative government cannot escape this decline to arbitrary rule unless, rather than merely acceding to the preference of the majority, it deliberately incorporates the cause of justice in the political order.

According to the Christian doctrine of the sovereignty of God, the ultimate principles of ethics are derived from the will of God; further, man's entire moral endeavor must be set within the purposes of God. While sovereignty of the democratic state is in principle just as objectionable as ultimacy of the dictatorial state, yet modern democratic ideals have often

---

[19] C. J. Friedrich, *The New Image of the Common Man* (Boston: Beacon Press, 1950), p. 41.
[20] E. L. Long, Jr., *Conscience and Compromise* (Philadelphia: Westminster Press, 1954), p. 7.
[21] Berggrav, *op. cit.*, pp. 101f.

received unqualified ecclesiastical commendation. S. Parkes Cadman appropriately warned: "Protestantism which accepts the challenge of the New Testament Faith must always resist theories that insist on the sovereignty of the democratic State as the organ of the Popular Will."[22]

Yet its lack of any ruling will, hence its potential anarchy, is the patent weakness of democratic government. Modern Socialism, according to Martin Buber, likewise promotes a new order of society wherein "everything is subordinated to conscious human will, indeed . . . designed as though there were no other factors at work than conscious human will."[23] Not only Communism but every non-theistic theory of society which deposes God as an authoritative lawgiver is driven finally to stress the complete regulatory power of government.[24]

(5) National life always has a distinctive character. The State is not merely an impersonal conglomeration of individual interests wherein personal rights are simply balanced and adjusted. The religious man believes that God's governance of the world includes civil government, and that through the nations God achieves certain of his purposes for mankind. Confidence that rulers exert civil power by God's providence, and that by rendering to Caesar what is Caesar's Christians show obedience to Caesar's Lord and to theirs, clarifies the nature of political responsibility for the believer.

6. THE STATE'S OBLIGATION TO JUSTICE

The decline of democratic ideals, as Professor Quick senses, follows inevitably from the modern failure to champion justice as actively as freedom. "It is a disaster that the democratic

22 S. P. Cadman, *Christianity and the State* (New York: Macmillan, 1924), p. 329.
23 M. Buber, *Paths in Utopia* (Boston: Beacon Press, 1949), p. 8.
24 T. R. Ingram, *The World Under God's Law* (Houston: St. Thomas Press, 1962), p. 121.

reformers of the last 150 years should have inscribed 'liberty' instead of 'justice' upon the banners of their movement," he comments. "True liberty is found only in the gospel, as St. Paul knew well. Apart from the gospel, liberty as a human ideal is a will-o'-the-wisp leading straight into the bog of individualism out of which men stumble painfully into the deeper morass of totalitarian oppression. But justice, even apart from the gospel, is a genuine light, to follow which is to set foot on a hard road towards the house of repentance. In social reform the Christian's task is to bring to the cause of justice the religious devotion without which that cause is lost."[25]

Until modern times the predominant view of government in Western civilization was that objective moral law limits the State's rights both in relation to its own subjects and to the outside world. The source of this emphasis on limited government power, as L. E. Elliott-Binns notes, is "to be found in the teaching of Christianity."[26]

In the early part of our century Raymond Calkins remarked: "The Christian idea of the State is that of the State as a servant. A servant State! How far it is from the minds of even the rank and file of Christian people! Here, evidently, is an area in the field of modern life which has not been penetrated, much less entered and occupied by the Christian Idea."[27] If the Christian view of the State as the servant of eternal justice found little acceptance in 1918, in our time the international trend has certainly relegated this emphasis to the outermost periphery of political theory. The history of the world in this century is likely to be conditioned by the moral ideals of the big powers fully as much as by any other agency of human influence.

[25] Quick, *op. cit.*, p. 60.
[26] L. E. Elliott-Binns, *Reconstruction: The Church's Part* (London: Frederick Muller, 1942), p. 36.
[27] R. Calkins, *The Christian Idea in the Modern World* (Boston: The Pilgrim Press, 1918), p. 85.

89

Fortunately, the American founding fathers did not equate representative government with Christianity, as if religious sanction exists exclusively for this one political system. But they clearly saw that democracy could be preserved from declining to relativism only within the context of justice. They avoided basing a free society on liberty alone, and set equality of freedom in the context of a just social order. They stressed man's unique relationship to the Creator as the bearer of an inalienable dignity, and affirmed the divine source and sanction of human rights as an emphasis indispensable to sound political theory. Frank Chodorov writes: "In all political science hitherto known it had been an axiom that rights were privileges handed down to subjects by the sovereign power. . . . A new king or a new parliament could abrogate existing rights or extend them to other groups or establish new favorites."[28] The early American political documents not only stress the limited power of the State, but also, in line with clear scriptural principles, incorporate an emphasis on man's possession of inalienable rights as a creature of God.

7. THE SUPERNATURAL GROUND OF JUSTICE

The Church upholds transcendent law in its insistence on man's dignity and on social morality, not for the sake of law as such, but in recognition of the centrality of God's revealed will. The Church knows the Lord who transcends all legal statutes and authority. It knows that law and religion meet in the law-enlightened conscience.

Only when a nation knows that law derives its secret power from the divine spiritual realm, from justice conceived as a supernatural perfection, only then is its respect for law secure. Even heathenism in the pagan nations of antiquity did not efface the connection of law with the supernatural world. The Apostle Paul's reference to the law inscribed on the

28 F. Chodorov, *One Is a Crowd* (New York: Devin-Adair, 1952) , p. 44.

conscience of the Gentiles (Rom. 2:15f.) reminds us that for all its pursuit of pagan gods, heathendom still had to reckon with a living sense of the transcendent basis of morality. It was the Christian Gospel that effectively set aside the ancient pagan myths, and cleansed and strengthened the sullied awareness of the living God's relationship to law and morality. Small wonder, then, that leaders of the enlightened nations could no longer accept as convincing or conceivable the ancient pagan supports of justice. But the contemporary failure to lay hold of biblical realities has again produced nations that are ignorant of the Christian revelation. Modern nations seek to support law on a basis that veritably negates the sacred and divine, something never before attempted in the history of civilization. The tendency to honor law merely as an expression of the will of the majority (of the moment) rather than an assessment of justice and law in, through, and under the will of God brings widening disrespect for law, and lawlessness in turn. Only when the State recognizes that statute laws are not the only law, that therefore statute laws are to be obeyed for some reason beyond their mere reality and character as statute laws, can the mood of autonomy be punctured. Only then will human law be revered as based on the divine order. A draft issued by the Christian Union of Professional Men of Greece shows the singular ability of Christianity to set law and justice convincingly in this supernatural context: "The fight for justice is a Christian fight in which only Christianity can provide a hope of success, because it uses the divine will as a basis for this fight, as a criterion for the existence of the Law, and as a superior foundation, which does not make the Law dependent either upon the subjective judgment and arbitrariness of the individual or upon the interests of the stronger."[29]

The Christian draws his assurance of the universality of law

[29] *Towards a Christian Civilization* (Athens: Damascus Publications, 1950) , p. 200.

from Scripture, a universality attested by the law written on men's hearts everywhere (Rom. 2:15). And the Bible closely relates its teaching of the universality of sin to that of the violated law of conscience (Rom. 5:12). This universally valid law makes social order possible; it not only judges man's disobedience of administered law, but also his willful surrender of absolute moral standards to subjective desires. Recognition of an objective and transcendent moral law that makes a universal and absolute claim upon every man's will is an indispensable condition of social co-operation. So intimate is the connection between the concept of justice as a moral principle and its legal expression that, as Quick says, "justice is . . . inseparably connected with law and . . . unthinkable apart from it; for the very notion of rights and duties must express the relation of men to an authoritative law."[30]

8. THE IMPARTIAL NATURE OF JUSTICE

Justice considers every person a subject of rights and an object of duties — the same rights and duties that qualify all other persons under the same circumstances. For that reason justice in the State must express itself in general laws that are to be applied without respect of persons. The justification of civil law is that it *protects* my rights (and my neighbor's). Government is not the creator of human rights; if it were, man's rights would be relative and discretionary. The role of government is but to declare, to apply, and to enforce rights which are given of God and therefore inalienable. Statute laws against murder, theft, fraud, and arson easily reveal such rights. But even in other cases, where they are not at once apparent, the existence of the protected rights is nonetheless presupposed. The purpose of law is to prevent one person from injuring another; my rights end and become my duty where my neighbor's rights begin.

Social order, therefore, can be maintained despite varied

30 Quick, *op. cit.,* p. 1.

theological views simply on the basis of the common acceptance of law. Objectives that promote justice and restrict
evil are to be pursued with all who honor the universal validity
of the moral law. A Christian need not reserve or restrict his
co-operation in the politico-economic arena to those who share
his theological convictions; in fact, he has no basis whatever
for such a limitation. Concerted political action is not to be
conditioned wholly on man's response to the Gospel. Nonetheless the Christian knows, as Forell observes, "that universal
and absolute law is ultimately rooted in God's will for man
and the world. It is a means which God has established to
preserve order and to restrain the self-destructive tendencies
of sin while the church is waiting for the final consummation.
This is the political use of the law, and the Christian Church
has the duty to make use of this law in this sense in order to
contribute to the earthly welfare of man."[31]

The Bible views government as a means of preserving justice
in a fallen and sinful order. In Barth's words, "The Church
always stands for the constitutional State, for the maximum
validity and application of (the) two-fold rule [no exemption
from and full protection by the law], and therefore it will
always be against any degeneration of the constitutional State
into tyranny or anarchy. . . . In its politics it will always be
urging the civil community to treat this fundamental purpose
of its existence with the utmost seriousness: the limiting and
preserving of man by the quest for and the establishment of
law."[32]

The Christian movement therefore has a vital stake not only
in justice and law, but also in the legal profession as such. To
encourage keen young Christians to pursue law as a profession
and to serve ultimately as judges is no less important than encouraging them to enter the ministry or the fields of medicine
and science. It is noteworthy that where Calvinism has flour-

[31] Forell, *loc. cit.*
[32] Barth, *op. cit.*, pp. 35f.

ished it has produced not only great theologians but also great jurists. Although evangelical Christians in America have sponsored such commendable organizations as the Christian Medical Society and the American Scientific Affiliation, only with the very recent formation of the Christian Legal Society has a similar association arisen for those in legal careers. This seeming lack of interest in the juridical professions is in fact a sign of broad indifference to political matters. If properly oriented, an awakening sense of political relevance will encourage professional interest in jurisprudence as well as in political theory and service.

Important as the Church's necessary concern may be for justice and law for the sake of social order, and hence for the sake of all men irrespective of their relationship to Christ, the Church has also an important gospel interest in law. Where the claims of justice and law are obscure, there the understanding of redemption will also be confused. On the other hand, a nation whose conscience is sensitive to the objective character of justice and law and morality provides an ideal climate among the citizens for the effective preaching of the Gospel. The Christian knows that the promotion of justice, whereby God wills the preservation of the State, can and must be — not as an operation of government but in the task of the Church — a strategic element in evangelizing a fallen race. Professor Quick observes: "So long as the world remains unredeemed, the Church needs the State and its justice to bring men to the gospel and open their minds to its meaning. Men cannot respond to God's love unless they understand something of his justice: they cannot be under grace, if they have never been under law. And it seems ideally right that in Christendom society should be doubly organized, in the State which represents justice and law, and in the Church which represents love and grace."[33]

Although a complete demonstration of God's justification

[33] Quick, *op. cit.*, p. 64.

is something future, yet the Church's witness to justification becomes even now — through insistence on objective atonement — a witness to justice. Because the Christian doctrine of justification presupposes respect for law, it reinforces man's regard for justice as well as for grace. When the Christian speaks of duties and rights and privileges, he does so always in the larger context of the revealed will of God, and of a known divine law which defines the rights, duties, and privileges of all mankind. It is therefore theologically significant that the political emphasis on objective justice shapes an atmosphere wholesome for effective preaching of the Gospel of Christ, and that the spiritual exposition of the Gospel witnesses at one and the same time to divine justification and to objective justice.

Yet the Christian should be interested in government not only because it creates evangelistic opportunities, but also because it preserves the social order and promotes justice as God's will for the fallen race. In her mission to the world, therefore, the Church ministers to the State both by expounding the invisible foundation and the proper role of civil government, and by setting the conflict between justice and injustice in the larger context of the will of God and man's spiritual revolt. As Barth says: "If the Church takes up its share of political responsibility, it must mean that it is taking up that human initiative which the State cannot take: it is giving the State the impulse which it cannot give itself; it is reminding the State of those things of which it is unable to remind itself."[34] One may accept Barth's further declaration that the Church's distinctions, judgments and decisions in the political arena are "always intended to foster the illumination of the State's connexion with the divine order [without defining that order simply as Barth does, as "the order of divine salvation and grace"] and to discourage all the attempts to hide this connexion." No doubt the Church will prefer which-

[34] Barth, *op. cit.,* pp. 33f.

ever live option most closely corresponds to the content of its own faith and gospel. But it does not follow, as Barth would have it, that the Church's activity in the political realm should be directed toward "the molding of the State into the likeness of the Kingdom of God." The aim of the Christian's political activity is not to produce a utopia, but to preserve justice and promote order in a fallen world. Jacques Ellul expresses this distinction well. The Christian must plunge into social and political problems, he writes, "in order to have an influence on the world, not in the hope of making it a paradise, but simply in order to make it tolerable — not in order to diminish the opposition between this world and the Kingdom of God, but simply in order to modify the opposition between the disorder of this world and the order of preservation that God wills for it — not in order to 'bring in' the Kingdom of God, but in order that the Gospel may be proclaimed, that all men may really hear the good news. . . ."[35]

Philippe Maury, general secretary of the World Christian Movement, views political activity as a means of fulfilling evangelistic responsibility and includes the Church's political ministry to the world as a part of the ministry of the Word.[36] Maury's formal inclusion of political activity under the category of Christian duty is proper enough. The performance of civic duty may properly be considered as pre-evangelistic, as we have already indicated. The Christian approves civil government as a provision of divine providence to preserve justice in fallen society, and ventures political participation in obedience to the will of God. This activity shapes continuing opportunities for him to witness both to the Christian view of the State, and to the Gospel of redemptive grace. He must beware, of course, of impugning the moral integrity of all political leaders who are not Christians; in this respect the

35 J. Ellul, *The Presence of the Kingdom* (Philadelphia: Westminster Press, 1951), p. 47.
36 P. Maury, *Politics and Evangelism* (New York: Doubleday, 1959).

biblical use of the term "a just man" will afford him sound guidance. The Christian can testify to the regenerating grace of God, which, in contrast to sin's frequent corroding effect, shapes new sensitivity for righteousness and devotion to duty in the private and public lives of individuals. His declaration of God's purpose to preserve justice in the public order supplies a point of contact for attesting divine regeneration in his own personal experience. Moreover, the very drift of political events sometimes provides an opportunity for preaching the Gospel.

Yet it seems unjustifiable to compass all Christian political activity into the category of evangelism, in the technical sense of that term, or to require that all such legitimate political activity be justified as evangelism. Both political activity and evangelistic activity are properly motivated by obedience to the will of God, but each has a different content and different primary objective. Is it correct to say that "without political action evangelism is incomplete and distorted" and that "in political life we should never lose sight" of the goal of "the conversion of all men"?[37] The Christian may and should view his political activity as a form of spiritual service, and political action as also a form of Christian witness. But does this perspective imply an undifferentiated and unlimited politics-evangelism relationship? Certainly legitimate political objectives are not restricted to those which directly or indirectly promote the Christian conversion of the citizenry.

9. JUSTICE AND THE DECALOGUE

The Church's most important concern in regard to law and order is that government should recognize its ultimate answerability to the supernatural source, sanction, and specification of human rights and duties, and hence of government's limited nature and role as a "minister" of justice. This recognition

[37] *Ibid.,* p. 107.

97

implies a congruity between the social commandments of the Decalogue and the principles expressed ideally in the laws of the State. Ancient pagan legislators, interestingly enough, classified murder, adultery, theft, false witness, and lack of parental respect as punishable crimes, whereas today Communist governments encourage some if not all of these practices to advance their immediate political objectives. Also significant is the fact that the Decalogue does not distinguish between personal and property rights, but treats the right of property as it does other human rights. The Apostle Paul in Romans 13:8-10 instructs the early Christians that they will best avoid punishment at the hands of pagan rulers by keeping the social laws of the Decalogue.[38]

Calvin's theocracy followed the traditional distinction of moral, ceremonial, and judicial aspects of the Mosaic law. While Hebrew judicial law supplied a political constitution that expounded rules of justice and equity, it lacked the perpetual authority of the moral law; other nations were free to adopt their own laws (without regard to Israel's political constitution or judicial law), but on the basis of the moral law as summarized in the Ten Commandments. D. Elton Trueblood asserts that "The Ten Commandments constitute the most memorable and succinct extant formulation of the ethical creed of the West. . . . They provide a convenient statement of the fundamental basis of recovery and reconstruction" in a world wherein "the problem of moral reconstruction is the primary problem." He stresses the importance of "the total view of life of which the classic commandments are shorthand presentations. Each of the commandments can be greatly expanded; each can be stated in positive rather than negative form. . . . When this is done, we have . . . positive principles of such a nature that a good society can-

---

38 Cf. Jean Héring, *A Good and Bad Government According to the New Testament* (Springfield, Ill.: Chas. C. Thomas, 1954) , p. 19.

not be constructed or reconstructed without reference to them."[39]

10. SETTING A STANDARD FOR OTHERS

If the Christian's moral duty includes civic and political duty as well, the Church dare not be indifferent to the particular structures and patterns of political order. How, then, is it to acquit itself? What is the proper role of the Church in articulating political theory and action?

Every search for Christian perspective on political and social matters must identify righteousness as the New Testament's central interest, in contrast to modern motifs such as security and even freedom. Any reader of the Bible will readily note that political action and social reform are nowhere cited as a cure for the moral problems of humanity; the Scriptures emphasize, rather, the spiritual gifts of repentance and regeneration.

If, moreover, one sets the Old Testament commands and the New Testament formulation side by side, he is further impressed by the inwardness and simplicity of the Christian view of man's duty, even if love is held to fulfill (rather than displace) the commandments. The development of Christian character comes by applying all time and all talent with a sense of responsibility to God and neighbor. Responsibility for God-given time includes the Christian's work and leisure and sleep, his use of weekdays and the Lord's day; responsibility for God-given talent includes his trusteeship of special skills and his stewardship of possessions. Christ's disciple is to invest his time as a divine entrustment to the service of God and neighbor. Obviously a large portion of man's time is absorbed by the world of work, and elsewhere we have stressed the importance of dedicating one's work as a a divine vocational penetration of the social order.

[39] D. E. Trueblood, *Foundations for Reconstruction* (New York: Harper, 1946), p. 10.

The Christian is called not simply to abstain from evil and to deal justly with other men, but he is also to seek his neighbor's regeneration. Wherever his life touches human need, the believer is to respond. His involvement in social responsibility grows not so much out of a comprehensive social theory as out of direct obedience to God and genuine personal interest in his neighbors. In addressing the Lake Forest Consultation in August, 1962, on "The Christian in Society," Dr. Bruce M. Metzger of Princeton Theological Seminary called attention to the New Testament's setting forth of Christian truth in the letter-form of personal instruction. This warm framework of intimate correspondence as a vehicle of moral instruction may suggest, too, the importance of the personal approach in addressing the Christian message to the social order.

In a moving passage Dean W. R. Inge captures what every unbiased reader of the Gospels and Epistles must acknowledge to reflect the relationship of the early Christian Church to the world about it. "Our whole duty," Dean Inge states, is "to hold up the Christian view of life, the Christian standard of values, steadily before the eyes of our generation . . . to live by that standard ourselves; to show that we are not ashamed of it, that we find that it works, that we are ready to defend and justify it to all questioners. . . . We all know the unique stress which our Lord lays on love and sympathy . . . how He broke down all the barriers, sacred and profane, that separate man from man; how He made everything depend on inwardness — the moral motive of action . . . how He taught the necessity of absolute sincerity and single-mindedness; how He advocated plain living without harsh asceticism; how He transformed all values in the light of our divine sonship and heavenly citizenship. . . . We are to use these convictions of ours in helping to form public opinion, and in setting a standard to others. . . . There is no such lever for moving society as religious faith. It *really* moves society, just because it alters the will and character of individuals. There is no political alchemy whereby you can get golden results out of leaden instincts. But make the tree good, and its fruit will also be good. I think we have the highest authority for believing that this is the best, nay, the only true method of social amelioration."[40]

No doubt moral duty defined solely in terms of individual behavior is inadequate; in order to penetrate the whole of community life the demands of ethics must confront the powerful social institutions in the areas of business and labor. Yet, as Cunningham reminds us, "The coercive power of the State is effective within certain limits, but it has limitations: it can put down patent evil, and thus improve the condition of the masses. It can even coerce so as to bring the general level of life up to a given standard."[41] What the law cannot do, however, is to confer the power of moral obedience.

It was Ruskin who remarked that the truest and most effective legislation is that which every man imposes on himself. The aim of legislation, if men wish to preserve their freedom, should be to train citizens to live above the necessity for detailed statute laws. Legislation ought to express what the people themselves realize must be obeyed, rather than declare what people do because they must.

11. THE ROLE OF CHRISTIAN OPINION

But a portion of every believer's time is also divinely mandated in terms of political responsibility. This duty is not limited to those who, because they pursue governmental careers, find that their vocational and political activities coincide. In respect to giving time and talent to the State, the Christian's chief duty as a citizen of the community is that of civil obedience. Because of the local church's place in the

---

[40] W. R. Inge, *The Church and the Age* (London: Longmans, Green, 1912), pp. 81f., 88.
[41] Cunningham, *op. cit.*, p. 198.

community, concern for the political realm should reflect a sense of obligation toward its townspeople, and reflect also a desire to understand the implications of the Bible for man's life and work and leisure. Fulfillment of Christian duty involves much more than inviting a neighbor to church or prayer meeting; it includes inviting him to Christ as the Lord of life — not by way of evangelistic witness alone, but through faithful exemplification of Christian citizenship. The Christian is called to active citizenship; he is called out of detachment and into involvement.

The Christian's opportunity to create a truly informed public opinion offers him an open door to indirect but effective political influence. Stimulating a wave of popular feeling and public will for social justice and against social evils is not only a live possibility in the Free World, but is an indispensable factor in a worthy methodology of social reform. This man-to-man influence of dedicated believers is emphasized by Cunningham: "Christianity will work along the lines of least resistance if it appeals, not to society as a whole or to men in masses, but to individuals personally. The experience of centuries in the past, and of earnest Christians in the present day, furnishes overwhelming testimony to show that an influence may be brought to bear on personal habits of thought, which will affect all a man's activities both in his private relations and in his public duties. . . . There is no element of compulsion about it, as it is not enforced either by civil authority or ecclesiastical censures; it appeals directly to the personal will of the individual man or woman. . . . There was with Him (our Lord) no suggestion of enforcing a code on a newly constituted society."[42] In an address at Cardiff in 1911, Lloyd George told the clergy of all denominations that the proper sphere of church influence is "not to support particular parties, not to advocate a particular measure of reform, but to create an atmosphere in which

[42] *Ibid.,* pp. 222ff.

it will be impossible for anybody to remain a ruler of the realm unless he deals with those social problems. . . . The first thing we have got to do is to create a temper, a spirit, an atmosphere that will compel men of all parties to deal with these problems, whichever party is in power for the time being. . . . The function of the Church is not to engage in party brawls. It is not to urge any specific measures. It is to create an atmosphere in which the rulers of this country, whether in the Legislature or the municipalities, not only can engage in reforming these dire evils, but in which it will be impossible not to do so."[43]

J. Clifford Gill remarks that "an upsurge of well-informed Christian opinion would give a new direction to social and political life."[44] An effective way to register Christian influence on the social scene is for Christian individuals to expose and assail particular abuses at the local level, and to widen the moral demand for their correction. Public conscience must be aroused not simply to the existence of social evils, but also to the need of just and right alternatives. The opportunity for personal influence in shaping public opinion, however, suggests the importance of not turning immediately to public compulsion to rectify community evils. Amid the widespread modern reliance on coercive pressures and legislative action for remedial measures, churchgoers must not underestimate the value and power of personal conference and discussion. Unfortunately, public opinion is more easily aroused to demands for political action than to appeals for the personal self-discipline and moral earnestness so necessary in a sound social order.

The real key to the spirit even of large institutions is usually found in a small group of individuals who act corporately. And government coercion, as Cunningham adds, "has very

[43] *The Times* (London) (Dec. 30, 1911), p. 5.
[44] J. Clifford Gill, *Christian Faith and Social Order* (Pamphlet; London: SPCK, 1948), p. 11.

little power of taking an initiative or acting as a pioneer. This can be best done by individuals; and the history of social improvement of every kind shows that individuals, who cherished a high ideal or had a strong sense of duty, have made a new departure which public bodies have been gradually persuaded to follow. While the State is powerless in this matter and may even narrow the scope of individual action, Christianity can bring an enormous influence to bear on individual lives personally. It can set before them high ideals for human life both personally and socially, and it can stimulate a sense of duty. This is the special work which Christianity has done in the past, and is doing at the present day, and there is no other doctrine which can claim to do it more effectively."[45]

45 Cunningham, *op. cit.,* pp. 198f.

IV. THE CHRISTIAN STAKE IN
LEGISLATION:
PRACTICAL CONSIDERATIONS

THE CHURCH'S MISSION IN THE WORLD IS SPIRITUAL. ITS influence on the political order, therefore, must be registered indirectly, as a by-product of spiritual concerns. The Church as an organized movement must not allow its own energies to deteriorate into direct political activity, but must encourage its individual members to fulfill their political duties as a spiritual responsibility.

Former Congressman Brooks Hays has remarked that the minister of the Gospel best preserves his spiritual leadership by filling the role of mediator rather than by becoming partisan in political matters. A pastor may encourage discussion of political issues by church members without turning his pulpit over to political matters, without encouraging the congregation to adopt specific resolutions on political issues, without circulating petitions for signature, without personal participation in political forums, without promoting the false impression that the denominational board of social concerns speaks the mind and will of the entire denomination and without requiring his people to take a specific position in party politics. And in no case ought the Church — except perhaps in the most extreme emergencies — directly to address government, as one corporate body speaking to another, in political matters.[1]

[1] The emphasis of the Westminster Confession of Faith is noteworthy: "All synods and councils since the apostles' times, whether general or

Today Christian social action is often so defined as to include the proposing and drafting of legislation, its direct promotion by association with and membership in agencies organized for legislative objectives, and direct lobbying. Thus political action in virtually every sense becomes a function of the Church as a corporate entity, despite the fact that this is not the task for which ecclesiastical bodies sprang into existence, and despite the fact that the federal government grants tax exemption because churches are organized for religious purposes rather than for corporate political activities.

The clergy do not speak with the same competence and authority in practical politics as they do in spiritual and moral affairs. Ordination to the ministry does not automatically qualify a person to decide detailed politico-economic issues whose complexity frequently demands technical knowledge. The dignity of the Church is damaged when ecclesiastical leaders appear before political bodies to plead special cases in areas where churchmen obviously lack the information necessary to reach a sound political judgment, as in the case of disarmament policy. Too often what passes for authentic Christian social action is simply the local endorsement of commitments made by top-level denominational leaders on debatable legislative matters.

The local church must tolerate no antagonism or division between so-called "political actionists" and "prayer warriors." Prayer for rulers reminds all Christians of their duties as citizens; it reminds them also that the will of the Living God brackets the role of government, that political activity is not to displace spiritual dynamisms. Church members will thus

---

particular, may err, and many have erred; therefore they are not to be made the rule of faith or practise, but to be used as a help in both.

"Synods and councils are to handle or conclude nothing but that which is ecclesiastical: and are not to intermeddle with civil affairs which concern the commonwealth unless by way of humble petition in cases extraordinary; or by way of advice for satisfaction of conscience, if they be thereunto required by the civil magistrate" (Chapter XXXIII, III, IV).

be put on guard against those who, despairing of the relevance of the Church's evangelistic mission to the political and social situation, trust political power instead to usher in a Christian society through legislative reforms. Political action does not erase the need for prayer and evangelism any more than converting men to Christ destroys the importance of promoting justice in the social order. The Church should stress not only the spiritual propriety of prayer for rulers, but also its moral necessity as an act of civic duty. The minister who finds it easier to endorse a legislative proposal than to give an altar call may not actually have both feet in the world, but he does have only one foot in heaven. No congregation, moreover, should allow its "social action committee" to speak independently of the whole membership in community concerns. It is sheer Christian tragedy, furthermore, if such a committee does not represent the local church's deepest spiritual drives.

If Maury is right, that "it is the task of the church itself, in its institutional form," that is, of the church bodies, "to state in solemn, official and public pronouncements what God may have to say in the world about present political events," and that Christians in turn owe special respect to such declarations, his appended qualification is of utmost importance. Such pronouncements, he adds, "must be submitted to the biblical criterion"; if substantial agreement is lacking between church members over such pronouncements then the question is properly raised whether the biblical teaching has been correctly understood or applied.[2] The Church's guidance in socio-political matters is nullified unless its statements to church members are guided in turn by scriptural principles. Denominational leaders may indeed draw up sets of recommendations for their churches, provided they are received and understood not as the view of the entire church body nor as an infallible view from which nobody may differ in good

2 P. Maury, *Politics and Evangelism* (New York: Doubleday, 1959), pp. 68, 69.

conscience, but only as the best wisdom of those leaders at that time, intended simply for the guidance of the local members, which some or even most may reject and yet remain faithful and wise members of their churches. Some churchmen contend that although the entrenched leadership may not actually be right or best, a group of socially alert persons — whether the hierarchy or its opponents — ought always to be calling Christian people to social concern and action. But this proposal perpetuates the danger that "officially approved" political positions will be lobbied into legislation by the corporate church, and it tends to neglect the real need of the local churches. The primary responsibility of the pulpit is to inculcate in the Protestant community a respect for scriptural principles. Church members have a right and duty, therefore, to search and study official pronouncements for their underlying presuppositions. When the institutional church ceases to proclaim prophecy and ventures to promote politics instead, it prostitutes its calling and forfeits any claim to spiritual obedience.

Before registering their convictions in the political arena, church members should indeed be encouraged to discuss and debate specific political problems among themselves as Christians. Few things will encourage wider interest in civic performance than Christian engagement in earnest prayer and in intelligent discussion over the social, political, and economic implications of the biblical revelation. Such sober initiative in fulfilling civic duties will furnish other citizens a wholesome example of commendable political activity.

1. THE CHURCH AND LEGISLATIVE REFORM

Many social problems today arise as much from attaching extravagant expectations to legislative reforms as from misuse of political power. Doubtless each proposed reform has something to commend it to the public — not least of all, the sincerity of its proponents and the existence of some social evil that needs correction. But political compulsion does not automatically produce "good" people, who, obviously, are an indispensable ingredient of a good society. Failure to recognize this fact is a common defect of many political programs. Rufus W. Weaver, long a District of Columbia minister, contrasts governmental methods and those used by evangelical religion as follows: "The government controls through an outward constraint; we control through an inward restraint. The government uses coercion; we use persuasion. . . . The government seeks to promote love of country for the country's sake; we seek to promote love of country for Christ's sake. . . . The business of government is to make good laws; our business is to make good citizens, who will gladly obey these laws and continually demand better laws, embodying higher and higher ethical standards. The end of governmental administration is equal justice under the law; the end of our endeavor is the establishment of the will of God in the hearts and institutions of men."[3]

Walter Rauschenbusch had envisioned the progressive regeneration of social life through the mobilization of latent moral forces. His followers, who pioneered "the new social Christianity," dissociated this vision, however, from the priority of individual regeneration upon which Rauschenbusch himself insisted. "The greatest contribution which any man can make to the social movement," Rauschenbusch had said, "is the contribution of a regenerated personality, of a will which sets justice above policy and profit, and of an intellect emancipated from falsehood."[4] Although Rauschenbusch thus stressed the indispensability of personal regeneration, he also encouraged the Church to participate directly in political affairs even to the extent of ecclesiastical lobbying for specific political objectives.[5] While Rauschenbusch protested against

[3] R. W. Weaver, *The Christian Faith at the Nation's Capital* (Philadelphia: Judson Press, 1936), pp. 39f.

[4] W. Rauschenbusch, *Christianity and the Social Crisis* (New York: Macmillan, 1914), p. 351.

[5] *Ibid.*, pp. 372f.

"an exaggerated idea of the importance of laws" and urged that spiritual vitality alone creates that moral power and enthusiasm[6] without which legislation cannot represent "any permanent and useful advance,"[7] he encouraged new political attitudes hitherto alien to American Protestantism. He believed that the Church should co-operate with the State in "creating the most delicate and valuable elements of social welfare and progress. . . . Their common aim is to transform humanity into the Kingdom of God."[8] Despite his preliminary insistence on personal spiritual regeneration, therefore, the "social gospel" viewed political action as a means not simply of promoting and preserving justice, but of actually transforming society. This social emphasis of Rauschenbusch's thought became characteristic of Protestant liberalism.

Since individual spiritual renewal was set aside as a requirement for social transformation, a much larger role (than they really could bear) was then almost inevitably attached to other agents of change such as education and legislation. Those who advocated "christianizing" the social order now intended much more than isolated specific reforms; while they meant something less than regeneration based in the supernatural renewal of individual persons, they spoke more of reconstruction than of simple reformation. Soon "social evangelization" became synonymous with idealistic political action, and centered increasingly in ecclesiastical pressures inspired by denominational hierarchies and implemented by their political lobbies. Thus dynamisms originally intended to *preserve* social order were assigned the additional expectation of *transforming* the social order, and their wholly proper and indispensable role was distorted. Reliance on social legislation as a moral dynamic was now promoted at the expense of spiritual alternatives, and in contrast with legislation the latter were

6 *Ibid.,* p. 373.
7 *Ibid.,* p. 376.
8 *Ibid.,* p. 380.

disregarded as inferior methods of securing social objectives. Kathleen W. MacArthur, for example, asks, "Can we . . . think what a big step forward could be taken if we could get international laws that would work, instead of threats of war and war itself?"[9] In the long run, this attachment of excessive expectations to the *preserving* dynamisms could only lead to disillusionment, and to a subsequent distrust of their adequacy not only for social regeneration (for which they never were intended) but even for preservation of social order (in which they have an essential role).

As Protestant liberalism dissolved confidence in the distinctive supernaturalism of Christian redemption, emphasis shifted to those latent forces which Christianity was said to share with other religions and which co-operatively could transform the social order. Offering assorted figures of speech just where literal guidance was most needed, S. Parkes Cadman, onetime president of the Federal Council of Churches, championed the new social crusade this way: "Should Protestantism direct its onpressing energies against open wrongs, it can, with the help of all believers in justice, clear the economic jungles of its beasts of prey . . . . Yet . . . the new social order is not to be ushered in by blows, nor hewn out after the fashion of the sword nor tempered on anvils of steel. Those who shall introduce it, Jew or Gentile, Catholic or Protestant, must stand, Godward and together, interpreting its requirements with the vision of faith, with 'the patience of passion,' with 'the signet of love for a seal.' "[10]

The author of the authorized biography *Walter Rauschenbusch*, D. R. Sharpe, pointedly expressed the general idea of a political Christianity in the chapter titled "The Church Must Strive to Realize the Will of God in Society."[11]

[9] K. W. MacArthur, *The Bible and Human Rights,* rev. ed. (New York: The Woman's Press, 1949) , p. 87.
[10] S. P. Cadman, *Christianity and the State* (New York: Macmillan, 1934) , p. 331.
[11] D. R. Sharpe, *Call to Christian Action* (New York: Harper, 1949) .

Executive secretary of the Cleveland Baptist Association for many years, Dr. Sharpe declared that "the Church must maintain an undying determination to get the will of God realized in the organized life of every community and to see the life of Christ reflected in every man and woman. . . . The coming Kingdom is the progressive realization of the ideal of Jesus in the individual and in society. Hence every aspect of corporate as well as individual life must be brought into accord with the law of divine justice, mercy and love. Each family unit, each social group, each purposive association, the economic life, the state, the nation, the world must be brought into captivity to the divine will. . . . Christian socialism, co-operatives, world missions, labor unions, the Church, the home, or anything else that advances the cause of justice, liberty, equality, and fraternity in the world, means the advance of the Kingdom of God. . . ."[12] The Kingdom of God he defines as "the organization of the total of human society in obedience to the loving will of God."[13] Although Jesus had said "Except a man be born again he cannot see the Kingdom of God," Dr. Sharpe tells us rather that we are in sight of "The Beloved Community" when all people — irrespective of race, color or creed — are guaranteed "equal educational opportunities; equal economic and employment opportunities; equal chance for decent housing; equal health protection and care; equal cultural advantages; equal use of the radio, television and press; equal recreational opportunities; . . . equal personal and social status," and so on.[14] The Church therefore is assigned the challenge of bringing the Kingdom of God on earth by promoting what Dr. Sharpe alternately calls Christian democracy or a Christian co-operative Commonwealth.

Whenever the Church considers itself the conscience of the

12 *Ibid.*, pp. 112ff.
13 *Ibid.*, p. 117.
14 *Ibid.*, p. 122.

State, or the pulsebeat of the body politic, the damage it incurs by thus directly merging its interests with those of the world or the surrounding culture is no less serious than that inflicted on a political order by the Church's legislation of her patterns of social behavior upon society in general. Such compulsion or coercion of free persons for "the common good" is not peculiar to Roman Catholic political strategy; in even more subtle ways it characterized the program of Protestant liberalism that maneuvered its way into phases of American national life. In 1937 John T. McNeill reflected this modernist dream of a christianized society by saying: "Liberalism shows itself more influential in long trends of social development than in the sudden crises when brute force comes into play. Its function is to leaven thought and life with attitudes and principles that make improbable the occurrence of such violent crises."[15] Speaking for the Federal Council, predecessor of the National Council of Churches, S. Parkes Cadman declared that "the imperative duty of Protestantism is world peace."[16] Apparently in utter disregard of Jesus' contrast of Christian peace with world peace ("my peace I give unto you: not as the world giveth. . ."; John 14:27) Cadman added: "There can be no moral or spiritual growth in nations till the causes of war are abolished by a united Christian consciousness. All Churches should organize and act for this end. . . . They should require the political authorities of their respective nations to define and codify international law. . . . Peace and war are primarily states of mind." The "heavy end" of the task of "world reconstruction" was assigned to those historic Churches which have bred great nations and fostered their sense of superiority. "The ultimate goal of nations is . . . Christianized Brotherhood."[17]

---

[15] J. T. McNeill, *Christian Hope for World Society* (Chicago: Willett & Clark, 1937), p. 256.
[16] Cadman, *op. cit.*, p. 327.
[17] *Ibid.*, pp. 327, 329.

Not wholly dissimilar is the confidence expressed by leaders of the YMCA; the Church, they indicate, is to venture "the reconstruction of society" by adapting social relationships and institutions so that they will be truer expressions of God's purpose for the world."[18] Significantly enough the organization's leaders state: "The YMCA, by its very nature as a Christian fellowship which includes persons of varying social backgrounds and political points of view, can seldom if ever be an advocate of a particular system or a specific legislative proposal; but it can and should inspire and equip its members to make a choice as Christians between different social attitudes and political policies, and to support effectively those which they have chosen."[19] In actual practice, however, the social gospel was to lend more and more institutional support to specific proposals.

Ecclesiastical leaders who increasingly approve legislation as a means of securing a Christian society, and social action committees that promote social renewal by political compulsion, seldom squarely analyze this technique. The use of political compulsion to regenerate society is alien both to American political traditions and to the Protestant religious heritage. Confusion in this regard is illustrated in Dr. Arthur S. Flemming's remarks in opening the 1950 National Study Conference on the Church and Economic Life sponsored by the Federal Council of Churches. A leading Methodist serving Ohio Wesleyan University as president, Dr. Flemming urged selected churchmen active in labor, management, economics, and theology, to "point the way to solutions that will rest on a sound understanding and appreciation of the facts of our economic life and that will be consistent with His law of love. . . . There are conflicts between the teachings of

[18] *Fellow Workmen for God,* A Guide to Study and Discussion for the XXII World Conference of the World's Alliance of Young Men's Christian Association (Geneva: World's Alliance of YMCA's, 1955), p. 71.
[19] *Ibid.,* p. 80.

Christ and the commonly accepted methods of dealing with the economic problems of our day. . . . Because we are followers of the Christ, we are determined to join forces in an effort to do everything within our power to really bring His Kingdom to pass on earth."[20] In his later role as Secretary of Health, Education and Welfare in the Eisenhower cabinet, Dr. Flemming's policies reflected a number of highly vulnerable assumptions now commonly held by members of church agencies that formulate denominational policy on politico-economic issues. These assumptions include, among others, that political action is a desirable way to implement Christ's Kingdom, that Christian love is normative for the political order, that broad public welfare appropriations are the preferable way to discharge the Christian duty of providing for the needy, and that patterns of economic security implemented along welfare state lines are anticipations of the Kingdom of God.

Does it really follow, as Forell would have us believe, that the Christian is "to do everything in his power to contribute to the earthly welfare of man by political means," and that this obligation is all the more imperative in a democracy?[21] While it is doubtless true that "the Lord will hold us no less responsible for our failures to use our political opportunity to serve the neighbor as for our failures . . . in the more obvious forms," does it follow, for example, that the Christian is to promote legislated government benefits as the means of fulfilling the Church's ministry of benevolence? After first urging that Christian duty be fulfilled as fully as possible through political means, it is all the more remarkable that Forell warns us against relying on political means to establish God's King-

[20] A. S. Flemming, "The Responsibility of Christians in an Interdependent Economic World" (New York: Department of the Church and Economic Life, the Federal Council of Churches of Christ in America, n.d.) , pp. iiif.
[21] G. W. Forell, "Law and Gospel as a Problem of Politics," in *Religion in Life* (Summer, 1962) .

115

dom, and notes that Christians suffer less illusion than others over the limits and ambiguities of political achievement.

As Protestant liberalism lost a genuinely theological perspective, it substituted mainly a political program. Much like those in Jesus' time who viewed the Kingdom of God as a political kingdom to be brought in by human power, liberal leaders required Christians not only to take a stand on political questions, but also so to define and direct political life that an earthly Kingdom would result from their remodeled earthly institutions.[22]

Those who profess to promote humanitarianism by legislative regulation, moreover, run the risk of defeating their own objective. They may, in fact, create public sympathy for a method of coercion which, when extended over all the interests of life, unwittingly encourages a large totalitarian restriction of personal liberty. Cunningham notes that before 1880 in Britain the public looked upon State interference as a sometimes necessary evil that should not be employed until all other alternatives have failed. Since the turn of the century, however, Britons have tended to view the coercive power of the State as a beneficent force that should be enlisted in preference to feebler instruments for redressing social injustices, and to hail government interference as "the best and practically the only method for introducing real improvement in the condition of a society."[23] Cunningham adds: "The seventeenth-century Calvinists endeavoured by means of Ecclesiastical Courts to coerce men into conforming to a godly polity over every part of which scriptural authority

22 These churchmen, who claimed to stand in the Protestant tradition, seem to have forgotten the example of Luther, who opposed vigorously the attempt of certain Anabaptists to impose Christian ideals on the whole order of society. Contemporary liberals, while they do not reject secular government in principle, nevertheless seek to implement sectarian ideals and even a new social order by skillfully manipulating legislative techniques.

23 W. Cunningham, *Christianity and Politics* (Boston: Houghton Mifflin, 1915), p. 179.

could be claimed. The Neo-Calvinists, with modern ideals of what a polity ought to be, are inclined to invoke state aid to bring pressure upon other people so as to force them to do their duties. Humanitarians are often content with pointing out the neglects of other people, and with saying they should be forced to live up to a different standard."[24]

As a consequence of this growing reliance on State compulsion, each special interest now seeks direct political power as the best means of removing social grievances. Even more distressing is the consequent decline of the sense of personal responsibility, and the feeling that whatever can be justified within the scope of the law is permissible. When duty is viewed merely as what the State requires, the sense of personal duty inevitably declines and the fulfillment of duty shrinks. The State usually can enforce only a minimal interpretation of what is right.

As Christian movements have joined in the clamor for legislated social change, the sense of individual duty has given way steadily to artificial and inadequate substitutes: private interest, class interest, national interest. Reliance on legislative compulsion has become so widely accepted that even erstwhile advocates of free enterprise now at times seem prone to promote special interests through federal coercion. In the long run, such broad reliance on government power does not really advance the interest of any citizen of any class, nor of the public as a whole, not even of sound government: it is doomed to disappoint the high expectations that the citizens attach to it. In place of a sense of duty to the community, it substitutes interest in the mere readjustment of special interests; on the larger national scene, each group seeks its own objectives at the expense of the others, however injurious this may be in the long run to the community as a whole. Cunningham is surely right in his reminder that "no readjustment of political maxims within the nation, and no

[24] *Ibid.,* p. 197.

creation of new machinery throughout the civilized world, will itself do away with jealousy and greed. The consideration of interests can never be a substitute for a sense of national duty and of personal duty; these deal directly with the cause of the evil and may thus effect a permanent cure. Both in the world at large, and in different countries where the sense of the duty of the community and of duties to the community is imperfectly understood, there is a danger that powerful interests will encroach on individual liberty, and there is little hope of progress in society."[25]

The greatest danger of this new approach to social problems yet remains to be noted. When the power of the State becomes the means for compelling people to do their whole duty, this power can easily be employed as well to force people to do *what is not their duty at all*. The State becomes the dictator of man's duties and rights. While it may not yet compel them to contravene biblical injunctions, it may exact from its citizens requirements that negate biblically-approved virtues. Instructive in this connection is the experience of Amish farmers of Pennsylvania, who refused to pay social security taxes because they preferred to assist their aged and to provide for their own retirement needs through personal initiative rather than through state subsidy. Instead of exempting them on grounds of conscience (if not of sound economic principle) from the requirements and benefits of the federal program, the United States Government sold Amish property at auction to collect social security taxes.

An observation by Oscar Cullmann might readily be turned against the Protestant social gospel. He remarks, "The Gospel knows nothing of that confusion of the Kingdom of God with the State which is characteristic of the theocratic ideal of Judaism. On the contrary, it opposed the theocratic ideal of Judaism with the same sharpness with which it re-

25 *Ibid.*, pp. 215f.

sisted the totalitarian claims of the Roman State." Even more bluntly Cullmann says: "The Jewish theocratic ideal is expressly rejected by Christianity as satanic. . . ."[26]

In the light of New Testament theology, all politico-economic characterizations of the Kingdom of God are in fact indefensible. O. C. Quick notes that "Jesus expressly disclaimed any intention of being 'a judge and divider' among men, or of initiating any reform in the legal sphere. . . . It is simply impossible to settle on grounds of love or of faith in the gospel what is a fair remuneration for labour, what rights of private property and ownership are to be safeguarded and what disallowed, what methods of trade and professional conduct are to be lawful and what unlawful. . . . The conscience of Christians, who believe in the Logos of God as the ultimate author and judge of all law, ought to be particularly alive to the manifest short-comings of actual laws and customs and to flagrant wrongs which they allow. It ought to demand and work for a radical reconstruction of the social and economic order. But it is a muddle-headed idealism which would make that demand directly in the name of the gospel, as though the gospel itself could be directly and positively expressed in any legally determined order of any kind. It is justice, not love, which is the ideal of 'the social order.' The more just the social order, the more clearly the gospel will be able to convict men of personal sin in the deepest and most hopeful sense."[27]

Dean Inge reminds us of the warning to the Church implied by Jesus' temptations. Jesus rebuked the lure of material advantages as a means of gaining popular favor (win the masses by striking a bargain with the labor party, by abusing capitalists and abetting strikes, by advocating schemes for the

[26] O. Cullmann, *The State in The New Testament* (New York: Chas. Scribner's Sons, 1956), p. 9.
[27] O. C. Quick, *Christianity and Justice* (London: Sheldon Press, 1940), p. 67.

forcible redistribution of other people's property). "I can recall no instance of a Church which has gone into politics and has not come out badly smirched."[28] "It is treason against our Lord, against His Church, and against the laboring classes themselves," says Inge, "if we secularize our message, and fill our sermons, as some are doing, with echoes of the class-warfare. It is treason to tell them that Christianity has repented of its 'otherworldliness,' and is now more worthily occupied with . . . strikes and free meals and poor-law reform. It is our duty to maintain that it is otherworldliness which alone has transformed, and can transform, this world. . . . Otherworldliness simply means the conviction of the immeasurable superiority of spiritual goods over material. . . . Let us hear no more of 'winning the masses.' That is a phase for politicians, not evangelists. There is not the slightest probability that the largest crowd will ever be gathered in front of the narrow gate. . . . Christianity always appeals directly to individuals."[29]

Cunningham, too, notes that "the difficulty about Christian principles vanishes if they are regarded not as principles for the organization of society, but as the basis of personal duty in society. . . . What is chiefly needed from the Christian point of view . . . is the exercise of a spiritual power to awaken individuals to a sense of duty and to inspire them to do it."[30] Christianity enjoins the conscientious performance of every duty, and motivates men beyond living just for themselves to the voluntary use of their privileges in behalf of others. A really Christian culture provides the law with "spirit, power and life" and creates a kind of social life that is above the law, based on love and sacrifice.

The Christian view of society does not require forcing the

28 W. R. Inge, *The Church and The Age* (New York: Longmans, Green, 1912), pp. 71f.
29 *Ibid.*, pp. 75ff.
30 Cunningham, *op. cit.*, pp. 24f.

fruits of regeneration upon unregenerate men. Rather, the Christian view seeks public recognition, in theory and life, of those principles of justice necessary to national stability. With this distinction in mind, Christian believers will know that their primary mission is to win individuals to Jesus Christ as Redeemer and Lord, a task not to be confused with mis-guided attempts to christianize the world order. If this con-cept is not understood, the Church will be lured from its real ministry of conversion, and in time little genuine Chris-tianity will remain. Because the Church has lost the sense of its distinctive evangelistic mission, the social disorder that pervades our time is not being effectively challenged.

2. THE PROCLAMATION OF BIBLICAL SOCIAL PRINCIPLES

Yet the Church dare not be interested in social injustices merely as an occasion for evangelism. She has a standing responsibility to the province of social justice. That responsi-bility is first and foremost the vigorous declaration of the great principles of social order enunciated in the Scriptures.

Widespread neglect of human rights as a comprehensive concern is one of the heavy penalties the Church has been forced to pay as the price of a social activism that neglects covering principles, and of social passivity that reacts against mere pragmatic programming. Most liberal churches virtually bequeathed to the United Nations, which arose within a setting of liberal Protestant enthusiasm, the task of stipulating human rights.

In the theoretical realm the result was distressing. While the United Nations emphasized the super-national character of human rights, it left their transcendent supernatural basis in doubt. Many conservative churches wanted a clearer formal emphasis on the supernatural (rather than sociological) source and sanction of human rights, but failed to supply a biblical alternative. The contemporary exposition of human rights sig-nificantly compromises the biblical delineation, perhaps most

121

conspicuously in the modern failure (found also in Communism) to view the right of property as a human right.

The practical consequences were no less costly. Politically active churchmen, who often make a bad habit of involving the churches directly in political matters, identified the witness of the Church with partisan legislative programs that confer a special benefit upon one segment of society rather than protect society as a whole. So, for example, the liberal forces repeatedly neglect the legitimate concerns of the "right to work" movement, while supporting the cause of compulsory unionism, promoting higher minimum wages, and approving other specific legislative proposals as if they had biblical sanction.

The liberal clergy were, however, nearer the center of legitimate social action when they took a stand against race discrimination and for civil rights and equal opportunity before law. The conservative clergy are not to be excused for indifference over racial discrimination, even though they may rightly insist upon a clearer formulation of the relevant principles. Some conservative churchmen sensed that something was wrong — although they were unsure what it was — in the constant liberal appeal to "the gospel" to justify political programs, and hence they were tempted to evangelize *rather than* undertake a social witness. They were right, of course, in sensing that the Gospel cannot be simply transmuted into a message of social justice. They were also properly disturbed over the fact that liberal churchmen encouraged local law-breaking as a means of law-changing, and that they were often insensitive to the convictions of their own parishioners. But conservative churchmen were wrong in minimizing the importance of the Church's witness to the social order.

Some evangelical pastors have, indeed, publicly preached and taught the dignity of the human race on the basis of creation and redemption, and have deplored cutting off any segment of the body of humanity. But in the matter of expounding the biblical principles of social justice, of exposing unsound theories to open shame, of openly challenging race discrimination and civil rights compromises, the evangelical churches ought to have been *in the vanguard*. They shared, in fact, the one great spiritual dynamic — personal regeneration and sanctification — which overcomes the inner dispositions of prejudice, but this resource was not effectively enlisted. Too often evangelical pulpits have neglected to emphasize those very divine principles of social life which they professed to defend in the face of liberal and neo-orthodox theological defection. Hence, in the absence of relevant preaching, indignation over statute-breaking ran deeper in the Bible Belt than a sense of guilt concerning the injustice of their own local laws. So Christianity suffered this defeat: many liberal and neo-orthodox spokesmen neglected biblical principles and transgressed community laws but responded existentially to the needs and rights of persons, while many conservative churches neglected principles and persons and pleaded only for legal proprieties and for the peace of the community church.

In shaping a climate of public opinion, the ministry and the laity need the firm guidance of scriptural principles more than sentimental ideals championed by modern social reformers. Propaganda for visionary platitudes such as world government, pacifism, abolition of poverty, and universal social security, attests the ever-present risk of baptizing highly debatable programs with the hallowed title of authentic Christian social concern. In our generation the pulpit often propagandizes for social objectives lacking scriptural vindication, relying mainly upon humanitarian sentiment. Surely the Christian Church is on the side of government and peace and social justice and it should pursue with unfailing vigor even those unattainable goals for which the Scriptures supply a mandate. But the Church can be for international justice without in Christ's name promoting world federation; it can be for world peace without opposing just war; it can be against destitution without promoting forced redistribution of wealth — unless injustice is to be fought with injustice. The reliance on political means to lift all the burdens of mankind — whether poverty in Ghana, overpopulation in Latin America, or whatever else — is characteristic of contemporary social theory in which secular concerns wholly replace the spiritual. The Church has no mandate for scrambling its legitimate task of promoting justice with the novel theories of social panacea, including the program of welfare statism. Such secular proposals, while claiming to promote social justice, tend in the long run simply to readjust the existing disorders along new lines.

To contemplate and perform civic obligations, the layman no less than his minister needs a clear conception of biblical principles and of their bearing on important socio-political problems. It does not speak well for the clergy when they approach political responsibilities simply in pragmatic terms with no comprehensive Christian theology of the social order. Nor is it a service to arouse congregations to political action only on the edge of emergency situations. Taken institutionally, the contemporary Church has committed itself pragmatically on many issues, only to discover its lack of a controlling philosophy by which to maintain a consistent policy of thought and action. Its sorry history of political involvement often reflects a concession to strange new theories about the Church's role in the world.

We have already stressed some of the basic principles specially important for the contemporary political crisis. These pertain to the divine source and sanction of human rights; the accountability of men and nations to objective justice and transcendent moral law, and the servant-role of the State as a minister of justice and order in a fallen society; the permanent significance of the social commandments of the Decalogue; the inclusion of property rights as a human right; and so on.

124

That these principles are seemingly absent from political theory, even in some circles where discussion has presumably proceeded on Christian premises, is undoubtedly due to the impact of the newer theories of political reform influenced mainly by Karl Marx. Among the penalties paid by Christendom for meagre knowledge of its own heritage is that the primary clash between Christian and Communist political theory did not become apparent even to certain ecclesiastical leaders until the Marxist theory had already perpetrated its subordination of the individual to the will of the State, its denial of the right of private property, its suspension of all human rights upon government decree, and its displacement of objective justice and transcendent moral law by whatever is useful to the furtherance of state policy. Too late the Church became aware of how Communism subtly (sometimes even crudely) undermines the Decalogue not only by rejecting property rights but also by legitimizing murder, adultery, stealing, and false witness, whenever such practices promote the interest of the Party.

3. COMMITMENT TO PARTICULAR PROGRAMS

Yet this general statement of the Church's obligation to supply moral direction to the world around it, and especially to political life, does not really touch the basic issues that vex Protestant churches today. What does the Church mean, or what at least should be the Church's intention, when it promotes moral law as a guide for national and international policy? For a generation a main dispute in Christian social ethics has been how Christianity, in current ethical problems, is to proceed from the revealed will of God to individual Christian commitment. Concerning this problem of "trying to bridge the gap between Christian insights and convictions, on the one hand, and concrete ethical issues on the other," Frank Bell Lewis asks: "How is it possible to bring the one to bear upon the other without some religiously illicit trans-

125

action? . . . This problem seems so grave, and so fruitful of error, that some despair of it entirely and conclude that Christian faith cannot be brought to bear upon ethical issues in any clear way. Others rely upon various devices: the concept of natural law, of the orders of creation, a scale of maxims to bridge the gap, an alliance with this, that, or the other form of moral philosophy. . . . But those who regard the Scripture as seriously as we, esteeming the biblical norm of conduct, respecting both Testaments, and asserting the infallible rule of faith and practice — for us these expedients appear as supplements, not substitutes, for the Scripture's law in which we learn the content of the will of God."[31]

The Church must not identify itself completely with any of the prevailing secular political, social and economic theories. But to avoid being dismissed as indifferent to the culture in which it exists, and to assure an informed rather than an illiterate laity, the Christian movement will need to evaluate the live contemporary options, and to indicate whether they conform with sound biblical principles. Precisely at this juncture of becoming politically articulate the Christian movement today faces both the greatest opportunity and the greatest danger in its long course of history since the apostolic age. The opportunity is created by the global political crisis of our times. The danger, on the other hand, comes from the fact that while the Church may recognize missions and evangelism as its primary task, and recognize its necessary stake in justice and law, it nevertheless may engage in politics, if not for wrong motives, then in the wrong way and for the wrong ends.

Having emphasized the importance of prayer for the State; of study of the Scriptures for principles of social ethics; of discussion among church members over the Bible's bearing on current options; and having emphasized the personal in-

31 Frank Bell Lewis, *Reformed Faith and Today's Ethical Tensions,* Inaugural Address delivered March 1, 1955, at Union Theological Seminary, p. 12.

fluence of believers upon their fellow citizens, we still face this inescapable fact: Christians have a vital stake in the specific laws on the statute books. Particularly under representative or democratic forms of government the Christian citizen not only has the opportunity but also the obligation to participate actively in the political process itself. The decisive test of genuine political concern lies not simply in developing political theory; it is found rather in transmitting theory into something concrete and politically relevant. Many churchgoers, unfortunately, are still immune to the sting of Mark Hanna's remark: "Your kind of people are all right in a prayer meeting, but they're no good at a caucus."

Evangelical inactivity in political affairs contrasts so sharply with the subversive exploitation of democratic processes that it indirectly contributes a setting where left-wing strategists can more easily gain their political objectives. According to J. Edgar Hoover, astute director of the Federal Bureau of Investigation: "The Red Fascists have long followed the practice of making full use of democratic liberties: elections, lawful agitation and propaganda, and free speech, press, and assembly. Their basic premise: Reap every advantage possible."[32] Mr. Hoover shows that Communist strategy includes legal as well as illegal maneuvers in its "tactics of confusion, retreat, advance, infiltration, and hypocrisy." It would be sad indeed if an evangelical corrective were to be inspired mainly by anti-Communist motivations, real though the Communist menace assuredly is. A larger view of political responsibility than this should inspire them to political participation.

It is misleading, however, to blame evangelical Christians alone for political indifference in our times. In many respects their inertia reflects that of the citizenry at large (in 1960 only 63.5 per cent of the civilian population of eligible age

[32] J. Edgar Hoover, *Masters of Deceit* (New York: Henry Holt, 1958), p. 194.

voted in the presidential election). Actually, evangelical ranks reveal some conspicuous exceptions to this general lethargy. Not only are Christian men and women active in political parties and alertly engaged in political affairs in many cities, but some — even if a disappointing minority — serve in state and national offices. They ought not to be welcomed only as commencement speakers or as panelists to discuss religion and politics; they should be heralded, if not as missionaries by vocation, surely as vocational missionaries. Nor ought the illumination of revealed principles to be lost upon their socio-political activity. The Christian politician, the Christian economist, the Christian doctor, the Christian industrialist, the Christian unionist, the Christian employee should now be "beating out the issues" in terms of Christian commitment.

In *The Uneasy Conscience of Modern Fundamentalism* (Eerdmans, 1947), I noted some of the widening demand of evangelicals to enunciate the socio-political relevance of Christian beliefs. A Commission on Social Action emerged within the National Association of Evangelicals which sponsored discussion forums at annual conventions. Without lobbying for sectarian benefits or promoting specific items of legislation, this Association, with the encouragement of the director of its Washington office, Dr. Clyde W. Taylor, has shaped an enlarging interest in government affairs.[33] Although this awakening interest has until recently[34] lacked a well-formulated philosophy of evangelical relations with government, it begins with the premise that while the institutional Church ought not to engage in politics, individual churchgoers must fulfill an active political role. While the Church is not to seek secular political power, its members may and must exercise an influence in

[33] Cf. James DeForest Murch, *Co-operation Without Compromise* (Grand Rapids, Mich.: Wm. B. Eerdmans Publishing Co., 1956), pp. 136ff.
[34] At its 21st annual convention in 1963 in Buffalo, the NAE adopted a rather comprehensive statement on Church-State relations after sponsoring a week-long study conference on the subject.

public affairs. At present an evangelical philosophy of politics is doubtless more frequently discussed in *Christianity Today* than in any other conservative religious journal. From such dialogue, to which these lectures may give added stimulus, it is hoped a more definitive view of evangelical political relevance, strategy, and action will emerge.

Some professors of political science in our evangelical institutions are uneasy over the increasingly-asserted thesis that the Church ought not to meddle in politics. This trend, they believe, comes just at a time when they are endeavoring to redress the fundamentalist neglect of the political arena. Their concern is both justified and unjustified. The warning against "meddling," we should note, is not aimed at discouraging evangelical youth from political careers and from the fullest possible political participation. It does seek to discourage, however, an objectionable identification of the institutional Church with political objectives. If professors of political science narrowly identify Christian social ethics with specific party objectives, and wholly endorse particular items of legislative reform as the Christian solution to social evils, then they, too, fall under the rebuke of "meddling." This distinction between political indifference and political meddling needs to be defined in the local church and in the college classroom; pulpit and podium alike should clarify the difference for church members.

Biblical revelation confines itself largely to ideal principles of social order; it does not commit itself to particular parties or programs of social reform. A serious approach to political responsibilities, however, must move from the norm of principles to involvement with personalities, parties, and programs in the given situation, and must grapple with their respective claims to serve the cause of justice and truth. Here the individual Christian must commit his personal support; but he has no right to commit the endorsement of the Church as a whole.

Jan D. Dengerink reminds us that the Protestant Reformers left deep traces of Christian influence upon the political realm and the life of the State, and refused to shun current political affairs.[35] While opposing the Roman Catholic union of Church and State, they did not refrain from action in political matters; they found no scriptural warrant for complete detachment from the political arena. Calvin, in fact, fought the Anabaptists, who contended that Jesus Christ has "nothing to do with civil authority" (*Institutes*, IV, xx, 2). Calvin not only dedicated to King Francis I of France his *Institutes*, in which he assigned a "most sacred" role to civil authorities (IV, xx, 4), but also extended his political counsel beyond Geneva to the Huguenots in France. Whatever problems may vex contemporary Protestantism in its battle over legitimate or illegitimate involvement in political affairs, a neglect of political duty by Christians is inexcusable.

4. THE INDIVIDUAL AND CIVIC DUTY

Since modern representative forms of government allow the citizen a life very much his own and accord him a full voice in the affairs of his country, political action is a possibility for almost everyone. Under these circumstances there is no justification for a Christian to shirk his political duty and to shrink from direct political involvement. Christianity is a minority movement in an evil world gripped by complex and powerful mechanisms of iniquity, but this fact in no way excuses believers from obedience to the Lord in political affairs. Much of political discussion and debate may seem futile — and much of it is. Mutual recrimination of political parties; exaltation of personal ambition and aspiration above the good of the community; bribes and scandals and immorality among some politicians, may discourage Christians

[35] Jan Dengerink, "The Power of the Reformation in Political Life," in *International Reformed Bulletin* (Fifth Year, No. 9, April, 1962), pp. 1-7.

from participating in political activity. And often political parties seem more prone to promote their candidates than to create the responsible public opinion so indispensable to the effective life of the State. Nonetheless there are still those political leaders of integrity, those officeholders who would willingly jeopardize their tenure in order to support what is right even if unpopular; there are many who deplore corruption in office and immorality in private life. The more that uprightness vanishes, all the more imperative is Christian participation in the political arena, for the Christian religion has unique power to maintain and foster a better political atmosphere. By bringing the sense of political duty to bear upon his own private and public activities, the Christian citizen may awaken a similar spirit in others.

Failure to cast one's vote in a political society such as ours is nonperformance of duty, but so likewise is voting merely on the basis of selfish interest or political prejudice. Withholding one's influence in shaping community conviction and public opinion may also be a matter of civic delinquency, for the rights of free speech and of a free press supply an ideal opportunity for full expression of evangelical thought and conviction. Freedom to participate in national political decision goes hand in hand with the duty to do so responsibly. Writing congressmen and other officeholders is a meritorious but only a preliminary assumption of political responsibility, and even this is sometimes regrettably delayed until "after the issue is settled." The Christian's political interest is thoroughgoing only when it perseveres with the decisive political issues all the way from the primaries to the ballot box. To judge candidates, irrespective of their positions on fundamental political issues, simply on the basis of personal vices like profanity, drinking, or smoking, is too naive; this diverts attention from political considerations and tends to make fetishes rather than convictions the test of political eligibility. Anyone who excuses himself from the need of understanding political issues, and foregoes an intelligent opinion of them, is not really worthy of the privileges of citizenship; he cannot escape a measure of blame for the political injustices and human misery that follow ill-judged legislation. Christians ought not and need not allow all strategic political initiative to fall to political bosses and undesirable officeholders, to whose subsequent political control they then are able merely to react. Nor ought Christian concern in politics limit itself only to seeking a remedy for the most obvious evils and be satisfied with token improvements here and there. As Dengerink declares, Christian political thought and action must not center merely in "a few special subjects, but in the inner reformation of political life itself."[36] Evangelical Christians face the obligation of rethinking the structure, nature, and task of the modern state. The Christian view, therefore, requires both a thorough understanding of the biblical principles of government and active judgments in political affairs. And it will be registered most conspicuously in a democratic society if young Christians, instead of being taught to avoid politics like alcoholism and adultery, are encouraged to regard a career in government fully as legitimate a Christian vocation as medicine and missions.

The weakness of democratic government lies in its tacit assumption that if people have access to vital information they will automatically make the right decisions. This premise overlooks two important things. First, man is preoccupied with narrowly selfish concerns, and second, he needs moral motivation to do what he knows is good and right. Because inordinate selfishness and passion easily overwhelm one's sense of justice, self-government requires spiritual direction in order to succeed. Precisely at this point the Christian message stimulates those virtues which contribute to political and social well-being. Even the authors of the American Constitution set their apparent confidence in man's political

[36] *Ibid.,* p. 6.

ability, moral capacity, and social sensitivity in the context of spiritual principle. They particularly emphasized government's lack of authority to legislate against man's divinely-given rights. But to proclaim universally valid principles and to incorporate them into national political documents and life will not assure an adequate expression of political morality. These principles must find reflection in the lives of the citizenry. And when properly comprehended and appropriated, the Christian message energizes those very virtues of community life which best contribute to social well-being. If regenerated men permeate national institutions with the truth and power of dedicated living, a "new order" of social life may be expected to follow. Spirited participation by dedicated Christians may very well introduce the fresh inspiration so sorely needed in the political arena.

5. THE CLEFT BETWEEN CLERGY AND LAYMEN

We have noted that Christianity becomes politically relevant only when biblical principles are aggressively applied in the political realm. But some of the deepest controversies in American Protestantism in our generation have centered in the questions of method and objectives. In other words, *how* is political relevance properly (scripturally) achieved, and *what* political aims are properly (scripturally) approved?

How to implement Christian principles in politics has created deep resentments and considerable cleavage between many lay leaders in mainstream Protestant churches and the General Board of the National Council of Churches and denominational social action committees. The American Baptist Convention, for example, lost its largest affiliated church (First Baptist, Wichita) in protest against the Convention's identification with the National Council of Churches, whose specific commitments on controversial political and economic issues have provoked widespread dissent. The United Presbyterian Church, USA, has been criticized by some of its largest churches for improperly promoting legislative programs without scriptural warrant, and additionally because the tenor of such political commitments is often on the left. The Chairman's Final Report to the Laymen's National Committee of the National Council of Churches is a well-known summary of such grievances. Congressman after congressman has complained that representations made by lobbying representatives of one or another board or commission on social concerns have not accurately and faithfully represented the outlook of affiliates of these denominations who belong to churches in his home district. When ecclesiastical leaders make denominational commitments, dissenting ministers and laymen hesitate to reflect upon the representative character or integrity of their national spokesmen, yet something demoralizes and damages the character of churchmen who cannot really identify themselves in good conscience with public pronouncements reputed to reflect their views, and who are reluctant to dissociate themselves from such statements through fear of being categorized as denominationally disruptive.

Protestant lay leaders contend that ecclesiastical social action groups become divisive when they confer church endorsement on legislative issues on which church members are divided in good conscience, and then propagandize these views as expressive of the social ideals of their entire denomination, and as purporting to be the accurately reflected views of their churches. American politicians are familiar with representative processes, and they know that ecclesiastical organizations often lack the requisite lines of communication with their membership. Faced with the practical choice of proximate political goals, churchgoers as a result are now disinclined merely to follow the decisions or recommendations of denominational social action committees, and are subjecting to sharp scrutiny the deliberations of ecclesiastical planning boards in respect to means and ends. The Rev. Sheldon L. Rahn, Executive Director of the Department of Social Welfare of the National Council of Churches, emphasizes that "the primary responsibility for social education in the churches [rests] with denominational boards of social education and action." But the NCC-related social action commissions tend to view tax-supported welfare programs as expressions of Christian compassion, and to hail the increasing state provision of welfare benefits as "a victory for the churches"; it is precisely this fact which has led some churchgoers to suspect that a socialistic theory of government and not simply the biblical ideal of compassion motivates their alleged ecclesiastical representatives.

Quite aside from the political prejudices of individual church members, and whether these are gauged accurately by denominational leaders, laymen today are concerned lest the Church lose its distinctive identity and mission by descending to the level of secular institutions. Both evangelism and social justice are within the province of the Church, it is said, but the clergy compromise and betray a spiritual trust when they divert the Church into political activity. There can be little doubt that the widening mood of anti-clericalism in Protestant circles springs in part from grass roots resentment of the Church's corporate political involvement by denominational and ecumenical leaders.

On the battleground of political decision and action the layman must carry the full share of responsibility. His political inaction itself can be a form of action, an unwitting approval of the *status quo*. According to his ability and opportunity he must fulfill his civic duty in local, state, and national activities, whose direction decides the quality of public life. By active means he must support and promote those legislative policies most compatible with biblical principles. He must distinguish and evaluate the live options as competently as possible from the standpoint of a just political order. Opinions, even devout convictions, may sometimes differ over what best advances justice and morality; in addition, there is the difficulty of assessing motives and of forecasting results. But this measure of confusion is compounded almost to inevitability whenever church members are urged to participate politically without proper instruction in the great social principles of the Bible, and with the guidance only of periodic pronouncements of ecclesiastical bodies on controversial issues.

This vulnerability of American Protestantism in respect to Christian social ethics has resulted in a lack of cohesive social influence. Ecclesiastical leaders have neglected the basic duty of instilling a respect for the enduring principles of biblical ethics in the mind and heart of the Protestant community. Instead, they have busied themselves with making pragmatic pronouncements on political matters in which churchgoers ought to have been conscience-free to weigh the alternatives for themselves. Individual Christian involvement in political activities and organizations, and informed debate and decision on legislative alternatives, are wholly desirable. But any tendency should be resisted which relies simply on the recommendation of ecclesiastical leaders to settle political issues and does not pursue a good conscience by intelligently applying scriptural principles to political alternatives.

In reaching a decision on specific economic issues, it is often exasperatingly difficult to say that *this* is the Christian position. Too often such decisions must be made within a framework of political and economic institutions which themselves can hardly be reconciled with biblical principles. All the more remarkable, therefore, is the tendency of many ecclesiastical leaders to approve specific and detailed legislation as Christian, when they might better advance a fundamental critique of certain pervasive contemporary practices. In some cases denominational leaders acknowledge their inability to pursue a consistent line in recommending legislation, but they take pious refuge behind their professed assurance that "the Spirit leads us." Is it not incredible that some churchmen, whose critical views of the Bible rest on the premise that in ancient times the Spirit's inspiration did not correct erroneous scientific concepts, should seriously espouse the theory that in modern times the Spirit provides denominational leaders with the details of a divine science of economics? What is most relevant today, and what in fact is most neglected, is the whole range of scriptural principles. The Bible does not supply us with any detailed blueprint of economic legislation for our age, but its politico-economic perspectives are surer guides to justice in our practical decisions than churchmen are likely to secure by lobbying for periodic pragmatic adjustments that take the contemporary political complex for granted. As Elliott-Binns concedes, it is "not the Church's business to draft detailed plans or to prepare concrete programmes of reform"; it can rise above the utterance of "mere pious platitudes and vague resolutions" by "a declaration of certain principles by which any scheme can be tested. . . . The Church must be prepared to furnish what may be called a social philosophy, a corpus of ethical teaching, by which all institutions and practices can be tested. If it finds itself unable to do this, then its influence will diminish and almost certainly fade away almost to [the] vanishing point."[37]

Since criminal elements often are responsible for organized and mobilized social evil, there is little question that co-operating forces of good can most effectively confront it. Just at this juncture, however, the temptation arises to involve the Church objectionably in the arena of political activity. Elliott-Binns thinks, and wisely so, that the Church's political activity "is best carried out through individuals rather than by any official action."[38] Yet he asserts also that the social principles molding Christian concern, if given practical effect, "must sooner or later involve the Church in political action, for most reforms can only be carried out by legislation."[39]

[37] L. E. Elliott-Binns, *Reconstruction: The Church's Part* (London: Frederick Muller, 1942), pp. 67f.
[38] *Ibid.*, p. 77.
[39] *Ibid.*, p. 76.

Usually he would restrict such church intervention in politics to the furthering of particular measures.

Harvey Seifert, too, thinks that the Church must go beyond an enunciation of general principles to the endorsement of particular measures; it must take "a position of concrete measures or proposals (including specific issues, ballot propositions, or legislative bills)."[40]   Otherwise, he supposes, the Church would remain "relatively innocuous in the day-to-day decisions from which history is compounded."   Granted, as Seifert insists, that "a certain specificity is necessary for effective education and action," it does not follow at all, we feel, that the only alternative to innocuousness is the Church's direct endorsement of legislative proposals.   Nor does this specificity mean that effective education of the laity is not best achieved by educating church members in general moral principles, to be creatively and freely applied to contemporary issues.

William Cunningham thinks that the spirit of the Reformation requires the clergy's "active participation in party politics, by signifying approval of the measures of one party, and denouncing the neglect of the other."[41]   Yet he concedes that ministers of religion are just as likely as other people, if not more likely, to use exaggerated language in political agitation and to impute unworthy motives to the opposition, instead of contenting themselves with the wisdom or unwisdom of political proposals.   This, in fact, happens almost invariably on the edge of ecclesiastical entanglement in political campaigns. When taking sides on politico-economic issues, moreover, policy- making bodies of large denominations, and special committees or boards of the National Council of Churches, so plead their partisan commitments in the name of broad moral idealism and spiritual concern that, wittingly or unwittingly, they imply that clergymen who do not share these endorse-

---

40 H. Seifert, *The Church in Community Action* (New York: Abingdon-Cokesbury, 1952) , pp. 165f.
41 Cunningham, *op. cit.,* p. 193.

ments lack social awareness and ethical concern. It is note-worthy that Cunningham thinks it "specially to be feared that the Christian minister who feels called upon to use the pulpit for political agitation, is going outside the terms of his commission; he has a trust imposed upon him, and it is his duty to declare the eternal truth which has been revealed to man by our Lord. But in connection with the passing of any legislation the questions which arise are chiefly matters of expediency, and of forecasting the probable results of the measure. These are at best matters of opinion. The preacher's opinion may be a good opinion, or it may be a mistaken opinion, but it has no pretensions whatever to be a declaration of Divine Truth."[42]

6. WHAT OF A CHRISTIAN PARTY?

Through its misconception of Christian social responsibility, the neo-Protestant social gospel has so involved the institutional Church in political entanglements that complete aloofness on questions of social order — an equally objectionable alternative — is now impossible in our lifetime. The whole Protestant movement must now confront the widespread politico-economic disorder in a manner appropriate to the Church. In this climate of reaction and reassessment, evangelical Protestantism faces new and live temptations in its effort to enter the political scene influentially. Some who call for political renewal seem to retain the social gospel's objective of Christianizing the nations, insisting only that the emergence of a "Christian nation" depends invariably upon the regeneration of most of its citizens. Others unwittingly borrow the prevalent notion that the nation is progressively Christianized as it widens its tax-supported programs of welfare benefits. Still others promote the thesis that only the election of Chris-

42 *Ibid.*, p. 197.

ian officeholders and the launching of a Christian political party can satisfy evangelical political conscience.

Representative of this appeal for Christian officeholders is former U.S. Congressman Jerry Voorhis, whose motivation was regrettably merged with fanatic devotion to liberalism's "social gospel." Christians fail in their duty at election time, he says, unless millions of devoted churchgoers "nominate avowedly Christian candidates for office, and support Christian issues sharply drawn and presented to the people for decision by Christian leaders."[43] The counsel of dedicated Christian officeholders should indeed be earnestly sought. And while Christian voters are not restricted in principle to supporting only Christian candidates for office, it is usually true that the moral principles of a dedicated Christian politician engender trust. That a Christian politician operates on a distinctive code of public and personal morality should be readily apparent; the public should recognize him as an officeholder of high moral dedication. It does not follow invariably, however, that a Christian candidate is best qualified politically. And it never follows that, when elected, a Christian officeholder will or should secure all Christian objectives in society by political means.

The Christian in politics, says Voorhis, cannot expect to fulfill all his deepest convictions. But Voorhis bases this restriction not on scriptural considerations but only on circumstantial factors, that is, in terms of population balances. The Christian's deepest convictions cannot be infused into political life, he says, "until all men and women in the nation have become convinced and devoted and thoroughgoing Christians."[44] We would reply that if this were the case, the Christian politician must wait until everyone concurred with him before he could sponsor legislation successfully. Such a

43 J. Voorhis, *The Christian in Politics* (New York: Association Press, 1951), pp. 20f.
44 *Ibid.,* p. 26.

situation, obviously, can never obtain. This approach fails to distinguish the Christian's sectarian objectives from his public support of universally valid principles of justice and morality. Even if he has actual political control, the Christian politician has no mandate for implementing all desirable Christian social objectives by political measures. Voorhis' basic error lies in his identification of Christianity with the (so-called) "full gospel with its inescapable requirement that our existing society be progressively transformed into one of genuine brotherhood."[45]

Dengerink implies that establishing a Christian party is the only means by which evangelical Protestantism can again become politically relevant in lands like the United States, England, and Scotland, where Protestantism still represents a large part of the population but is no longer a political force.[46] In the Netherlands, such a party, founded by Abraham Kuyper (later appointed Prime Minister in the first decade of this century), enabled evangelical Protestants to wield important influence in that nation's political life. In Germany, a Christian socio-political movement between the two great wars gained strong Protestant backing for a time, although its early spiritual motivation soon faded. In Norway, Sweden, and Indonesia, small Protestant-Christian political parties have also appeared. In the United States, current interest in a third party, at least as a temporary strategy, seems to be encouraged by the ever lessening difference between the traditional parties. Recent emergence of Christian political movements attests a growing uneasiness over the lack of Christian leadership in the political arena.

According to Philippe Maury, the emergence of Christian political parties in Europe bespeaks the decadence of the traditional parties and public disappointment in them, and expresses as well "a sincere and commendable desire for renewal."

[45] *Ibid.,* p. 29.
[46] Dengerink, *op. cit.,* p. 6.

But, he adds, this trend also reflects a well-formed anti-Communist and pro-Catholic strategy by the Vatican.[47]   Its effect, moreover, often results in forcing the older parties to support purely confessional causes, such as state aid to parochial schools.   Formation of such Christian parties, moreover, does not rule out infiltration by those who approve their program but deny their faith; it encourages the temptation of politicians to use church identification and ecclesiastical organization as vehicles of personal ambition.   Nor does it preclude the party's sponsoring a program that is only presumptively but not actually Christian, and clothing a purely political program with a theological role or religious symbol.   Moreover, such parties may endanger Christian unity, since they imply that those who do not endorse the political program are deficient in their faith.   (The same risk of elevating political judgments into ecclesiastical positions, one might think, would also discourage ecclesiastical leaders and official boards from making particular pronouncements on political programs.)

Maury himself objects to Christian parties, however, on a debatable ground.   He claims that the Christian view of history and eschatology does not allow for Christian civilization, and therefore a Christian party with its own political program has no legitimate place.   Christian scholars will detect here an overly pessimistic view of history, even if the optimistic excesses of liberalism are avoided.   Maury refuses to call a political party Christian even if its members are Christians whose political decisions, while not directly and logically derived from theological convictions, are illumined by their faith.   To deduce any one detailed political program from the biblical revelation is no doubt impossible.   But this is not the real problem of a Christian party.   Even if it takes its stand on Christian principles, and concedes the far from perfect character of its program, the Church, in order to "save face"

[47] Maury, *op. cit.*, p. 82.

142

politically, may become more and more involved in a political orientation of its primary mission. "A Christian political party tends inevitably to identify the mission of the Church in the world with the political struggle," and it soon becomes an evangelistic liability by making critics of the party into critics of the Church as well.[48]

The Christian is not precluded, however, from changing party identifications or even from establishing new political groups. Whatever his political affiliation or status may be, the real danger he must avoid is that of political confessionism, of attaching ultimate loyalty to a party and its ideology and program, rather than to Christian principles.

In years past, American evangelicals and liberals joined in supporting the Prohibition Party. This party exhibited two weaknesses; first, its program was too narrow; second, it sought to legislate morals in an area of social conduct where many Christians around the world themselves disagreed. To identify the Church with any existing political party is objectionable. Such identification would inevitably require the Church to support many causes which are of indirect concern, and some which are actually objectionable to the Church.

Religious bodies which disown any interest in a church party nonetheless often promote candidates on the basis of religious blocs. In New York State, state and city tickets as well as appointments to judgeships, have long been balanced between Protestant, Catholic and Jew, with the behind-the-scenes approval of political and religious organizations. This arrangement not only works to the disadvantage of Protestant evangelicals, since liberal leaders are much more involved and influential in ecclesiastical and political machinery, but as a "representative" arrangement it tends to oversimplify the religious pluralisms of the American scene. Not long ago five Buddhists complained in New York because the Bud-

---

[48] *Ibid.*, pp. 85f.

dhists hold no judgeship to represent them. Its worst feature, however, is that it promotes the notion that an officeholder at the same time becomes his church's representative in the political order, which is hardly the same thing as a sense of church identification. Some ecclesiastical leaders contend that this device holds temporary value as long as major religious blocs survive in the pluralistic American context or until society becomes more cohesive and less bigoted. But the propriety of the practice is open to question.

Once any group (whether religious or racial) gets an appointment or office on this special basis, it tends to feel that the post belongs forever to some representative of the same constituency. In American political life, no segment of the populace (least of all on religious grounds) ought to think it has a permanent proprietary interest in any public office. If a president (or supreme court justice or congressman) is to be considered the political spokesman for his church, on what basis — in the event of death — is a successor to be named? No political office ought to be viewed as belonging to any specific religion; all should represent the broadest possible community of interest. Regrettably, ecclesiastical self-discipline is increasingly scarce, and lobbyists for sectarian groups exert more and more special pressures upon officeholders to support favored positions and programs. There is an area, of course, in which any officeholder may rightly consider himself a representative of his religious community — in the protection of the churches against government intrusion, and the protection of government against ecclesiastical intrusion. But no American officeholder has the official right to speak for his religious group alone, or to represent his religious group alone, or to seek political implementation of the sectarian objectives of any or all religious groups.

American politics centers in the two-party system. Party government, therefore, is doubtless the most effective agent for political influence, although freedom to challenge the established parties is a strong incentive to their self-reform. To the extent that the two major parties are organized simply for the aggrandizement of political power, through officeholding and control of patronage, Christian conscience faces a challenge to recall them to a fresh concern for political and social righteousness, and, failing in this, is free to probe alternatives.

Formation of a Christian party would seem quite alien to British and American patterns of political life. Without sponsoring a new party, evangelical voters in some cities have gained local political initiative by nominating and electing independent reform candidates in the face of corrupt administrations. In other instances, without founding a separate party, their special support of qualified candidates has turned the vote to elect major state officeholders. As a rule, Christian office seekers must seek re-election through an existing party. Since local traditions and circumstances often determine their party identification, the matter of specific political theory may not appear to be as significant in such a decision as it really is. The point is, that as an officeholder advances to higher positions he loses identification with local considerations and becomes more closely allied with his party's national platform.

Irrespective of party affiliation, Christian politicians ought to evaluate and discuss political issues from the perspective of the Christian doctrine of government, man, and society. For Christian politicians, party loyalty must always be expressed with qualification. Christians venture into politics not simply to serve a political party, but first of all to serve God and their fellow men.

V. THE NATURE OF GOD
AND SOCIAL IDEALS

CHRISTIAN DOCTRINE IS A HARMONIOUS UNITY WHOSE MAIN axis is the nature of God. For this reason a correct understanding of the whole range of Christian faith and duty turns on a proper comprehension of divine attributes. How the theologian defines and relates God's sovereignty, righteousness, and love actually predetermines his exposition of basic positions in many areas — in social ethics no less than in soteriology and eschatology. Even the smallest deviation from the biblical view of divine justice and divine benevolence eventually implies far-reaching consequences for the entire realm of Christian truth and life.

1. RIGHTEOUSNESS AND LOVE EQUALLY ULTIMATE

It is important, therefore, to note the historic evangelical emphasis that righteousness and benevolence are equally ultimate in the unity of the divine nature. In accord with biblical theology, evangelical Christianity affirms that justice is an immutable divine quality, not reducible to a mere mode of divine benevolence on the fallacious theory that love is the exclusive center and core of God's being. Since righteousness and justice (no less than love) are identical with the very being of God, moreover, an obstacle exists to the divine forgiveness of the sinner — an obstacle removed by the Redeemer's atonement, and which if unremoved excludes the impenitent from fellowship with God and dooms him to final retribution. Furthermore, this equal ultimacy of justice and benevolence in the nature of God has fundamental conse-

146

quences for man in society. In the sphere of social ethics
it is reflected in the biblical emphasis that the role of government in the world is to preserve justice, with an eye on
human rights and duties as sanctioned and stipulated and
supported by the will of God. The Church's role in the
world, on the other hand, is essentially redemptive and benevolent, alert to man's spiritual needs.

The great fallacy of Protestant liberalism was its theological
discounting of God's wrath by losing or submerging God's
righteousness in his love. Schleiermacher considers justice
only a reflex of our sense of sin and evil; the function of
justice decreases and disappears, therefore, as Christ's redemptive work overcomes this sense of sin. For Ritschl, God's
righteousness is "simply the consistency with which his love
provides for the good of men." In effect, this dissolving
of justice into love cancels any separate function for justice
in the moral order of the world, shifts the motive force of
ethical theory to benevolence instead, and misinterprets love
as a universal rather than a particular manifestation of the
divine nature. Recent liberal scholars proceeded to apply the
implications of this reformulation of the nature of God to
such related areas of ethical thought as criminology and
law, by making every aspect of social concern an instrumen-
tality of love. The whole social order thus yields to the
indoctrination of *agape*, and love blurs and erases the fundamental distinction between justice and benevolence in the
politico-economic realm.

Neo-orthodoxy's critical reaction to these liberal Protestant speculations about God still leaves much to be desired.
Yet even the least adjustment of the divine perfections has
consequences for theology and ethics. Karl Barth concedes
that Ritschl undermined the significance of divine wrath in
the New Testament and hence subverted the New Testament
concept of divine grace. Barth's condemnation of the modern-

147

ist erosion of the wrath of God is carried forward by Emil Brunner, who declares that just when "dealing with the Judgment and the Wrath of God" the Enlightenment school and theologians like Schleiermacher "turn away from the Bible. But it is precisely here," says Brunner, "that we stand at the decisive point in the whole Christian doctrine of God. . . ."[1]

At what point, then, does neo-orthodoxy break with the modernist reconstruction of God's nature? To answer this question we must note that Ritschl advanced two premises: (1) The Old Testament does not dissolve divine wrath into grace but contrasts divine wrath with the gracious action of God (here Ritschl agrees with the historic evangelical view); and (2) the New Testament rejects the "Old Testament view" of divine wrath for a larger comprehension of divine love and mercy, and restricts wrath wholly to the idea of God's eschatological victory (here Ritschl abandons the evangelical emphasis that both Old and New Testaments distinguish God's mercy and wrath objectively and essentially).

Barth relates divine love and wrath in a "neo-orthodox" way. He insists that wrath has New Testament as well as Old Testament reality, but contends that apart from grace it has no biblical reality in either the Old or New Testament. Barth is on surer ground than Ritschl, therefore, when he asserts that God meets men in wrath and grace in the New Testament exactly as he met Israel in the Old Testament, and that Jesus' crucifixion is the supreme exhibition of this fact. Thus Barth formally preserves some of the elements Ritschl sacrificed, particularly the unity of the Testaments — the Old Testament witness to Christ and Christ's fulfillment of the Old Testament in the New. And in his own peculiar way Barth seeks to overcome Ritschl's virtual erasure of wrath

---

[1] E. Brunner, *The Christian Doctrine of God* (Philadelphia: Westminster Press, 1950), p. 168.

from the New Testament. God is "provoked to anger" by man's disobedience, says Barth.[2]

But neo-orthodoxy merely modifies and does not rectify the error of liberalism. It relates righteousness and wrath inadequately to the core of God's being, still subordinating them to divine love. Barth's doctrine of God makes righteousness and mercy, wrath and love, simply variations of the same scriptural theme. As Barth puts it, "We do not overlook nor neglect anything, if we affirm that His love and therefore His whole being, in all the heights and depths of the Godhead, is simply grace."[3] If the intention of such a statement were merely to affirm that each of God's perfections is identical with the whole of his being, that would be one thing. But neo-orthodoxy sees the attribute of divine grace behind every other attribute, and neo-orthodox expositors therefore misapprehend love, grace, and justice. So Edward Farley, for example, asserts that "all God's acts are acts of grace, even his judgment."[4]

2. CONFLICT IN CURRENT ETHICAL THEORY

It does not follow that the neo-orthodox approach yields a wholly uniform scheme of social ethics, for neo-orthodox theologians give divergent expositions of many questions in politics and economics.

Conferring in 1950 in Treysa, Germany, the study department of the World Council of Churches discussed "The Biblical Doctrine of Law and Justice." Can civil law and social justice be understood only through God's saving activity manifested in Jesus Christ, and deduced only from the love shown in God's redeeming acts? Or should the ordinance of civil power be sharply distinguished from the Church and

[2] K. Barth, *Church Dogmatics*, II/1, p. 373.

[3] *Ibid.*, p. 358.

[4] E. Farley, *The Transcendence of God* (Philadelphia: Westminster Press, 1960), p. 217.

the gospel? Opinions differed sharply. Contemporary Protestant debate on social order is in fact full of claims and counterclaims over law and gospel, justice and grace. But new concepts of international law are already being projected on these differing bases, each presumably supplying an authentic Christian point of view. While totalitarianism and secularism threaten to subvert the whole realm of objective and universal law, influential theologians in the Christian community are therefore divided and undecided whether (1) in the name of the gospel some "new" law or "sacred justice" should be imposed on the world; or (2) whether the gospel should vitalize a universally valid "secular justice" already inherent in the existing social order.

Whether all divine revelation is saving, and whether there is general as well as special revelation, are issues which brought Barth and Brunner into early conflict. Differing answers to these questions lead to differing expositions of the relationship of law and justice in the realm of government to God's revelation in Christ.

Championing the "Christological" basis of law and social ethics, Barth asserts that law and justice must be understood as having their source in the love revealed in Christ.[5] He regards the whole world as an aspect of Christ's kingdom, and to make the world reflect the lordship of Christ, Barth would rule it by the gospel. For Barth the *polis* lies already within the kingdom of Christ. Barth thinks of the God for whom the State ministers not simply as Creator and Ruler (as do Protestant Reformers and orthodox theologians generally). The State must be seen in the light of its final eschatological transformation, Barth contends, rather than only in the light of its origin.

Barth's critics agree with him that the State is not independent of God. They find no fault with the Christological basis of justice and law, nor with the theological relationship be-

5 K. Barth, *Church and State* (London, SCM Press, 1939), p. 32.

tween God's life-preserving ordinances and his purpose in in redemption. They protest, however, that Barth's social theory ignores the real difference between the divine sovereignty over the present world order and Christ's kingdom in the Age to come. While God is Lord both of this world and of the Church or community of faith, he rules world and Church in different ways, they say. Christ is not related to the world as Head to Body. He rules the world by law, not by gospel.

Suppose, as Barth contends, that the kingdoms of this world are truly parables of the kingdom of God; suppose that Christ's lordship over them is already actual and direct. Can Christians then deplore the intentions of wicked rulers? Can they express deep indignation over the totalitarian state? When totalitarian government inevitably assumes its pseudo-religious character, may the Church unmask it? Must Soviet churchmen endorse totalitarian government, and Free World ecclesiastical leaders endorse the "welfare state," as expressions of the kingdom of God? In the light of the "Little Apocalypse" of Mark's Gospel (13:19,22), where only the elect recognize the antichrist for what he is, where does Barthian speculation about the God-state lead us? Does not Barth's approach virtually require our approval of evil acts simply because God ordains all that happens — as if we should worship Judas for betraying Jesus, since Judas thereby makes our salvation possible!

Can it really be contended, moreover, that Jesus of Nazareth proclaimed a *wholly new* concept of law and justice whose source and content come from the Gospel. Or even that Jesus' "theological inheritance" is that of an Old Testament which depicts love as God's "essential nature" and which locates justice in the divine nature only by way of "emphasis . . . on its meaning as love"?[6] This is utterly futile. One

[6] J. Arthur Baird, *The Justice of God in The Teachings of Jesus* (Philadelphia: Westminster Press, 1963), pp. 42ff.

cannot deny Jesus' interest in the promotion of justice and righteousness, in order thereby to emphasize his mission of redemptive mercy.[7] Jesus did not attribute a redemptive function to the Old Testament commandments. The Sermon on the Mount, his most extensive exposition of ethics, reinforces the demand for justice. He did not overthrow the judgment seats of earthly rulers, but subjected himself instead to juridical procedures in his own trial, even suffering injustice at the hands of Pilate. And he warned of a future judgment of the nations when final eschatological justice would take the measure of civil justice.

The question before us is not whether the real nature of justice is discerned in Christ, or whether Christian believers influence the world by shaping higher moral sensitivities. These issues are not in doubt. What is in debate, rather, is this: Are we to impose the Christian way upon the world, and, moreover, on the ground that the Gospel implements a special theological ethics in socio-political affairs? Opponents of Barth argue that such a course of action cannot really be deduced from scriptural teaching; it confuses the distinction between law and gospel; it would deprive non-Christians of their rights before the law; and it supplies no objective criteria for deciding what shall be law and what rights there are.

[7] Joseph Klausner points to Jesus' refusal to divide an inheritance and concludes that "Jesus . . . disregards justice generally, even when it is a case of natural civil interest, free of all ill motive; he thus ignores anything concerned with material civilization" (*Jesus of Nazareth*, New York, Macmillan, 1925, p. 375). But this is too extreme a conclusion to draw from Jesus' refusal to become involved in settlement of a family controversy. Others have asserted that Jesus apparently abandons recognition of mutual rights and duties for the principle of *agape*. But do Jesus' appearances before Pilate and his few dealings with civil authorities warrant so sweeping a theory of civil relations? So, too, those who note that *dike* does not occur in the biblical discussion of civil affairs seem unjustified in their broad assertion that the New Testament is not interested in the idea of justice in the forensic sense of a balancing of rewards and penalties in the public life.

The Nature of God and Social Ideals

Some theologians in the United Presbyterian Church in the U.S.A., enamoured of Barth's theory that divine revelation is always Christological and hence redemptive, now oppose theistic affirmations in public institutions. They consider all such religious affirmations to be either meaningless generalities (hence to be avoided) or specifically sectarian (hence prohibited by the constitutional separation of Church and State). Barth's rejection of general revelation is therefore invoked, curiously, to shape a state which in public functions acts as if God were non-existent, and which gives no public recognition of answerability to transcendent truth and objective justice as these are established by a supernatural Creator. Yet some of these same theological leaders — in the name of authentic Christian social concern — simultaneously throw ecclesiastical weight behind legislative proposals that broaden the state's welfare responsibility. They presume to give to government a redemptive character under the supposed inspiration of the revealed will of God. Thus the distinction between justice and benevolence is blurred.

Recent discussions of "the two realms" of Church and State reflect an increasing attempt to adjust law to love. For the Christian both realms find their basic sanction and power in God, whose righteousness and mercy are revealed supremely in Jesus Christ. But theologians who view all divine activity, at whatever level, as an expression of saving grace, must also depict law and justice in terms of God's redemptive love. On the other hand, theologians who insist on the equal ultimacy of righteousness and love in God connect law and justice fundamentally with the ordinances of creation and preservation rather than with the order of redemption. They emphasize that the authority of the State issues not from the activity of Christ in redemption but from the activity of Christ in creation and preservation. They speak of God's common grace in distinction from his saving grace and maintain that this distinction accords better with the realities of righteousness

153

and love in the divine nature than does a subsumption of God's activity under the category of redeeming grace.

Unquestionably, today's social ferment can be traced to biblical ideas as well as to Marxian ideas. Many of the peoples of Africa and Asia first learned of objective justice and love through the witness and teaching of Christian missionaries. These concepts are now widely exploited by Communists (who distort their meaning), but we must not forget that long before the rise of Communist theory, and in fact even long before the classic Greek philosophers, the prophets of revealed religion declared that what the Living God requires of man is "to do justly, and to love mercy, and to walk humbly with thy God" (Micah 6:8). Yet contemporary theology so confuses righteousness and grace in the nature of God that justice and benevolence become mixed objectionably in social theory. Philippe Maury, general secretary of the World Christian Movement, ventures to instruct us that "in 1960, to love our fellow men means to engage in politics."[4]

3. THE DILUTION OF JUSTICE BY "LOVE"

World ecumenical statements on social affairs have tended to be fragmentary, lacking a general theory of social justice. A few, mainly neo-orthodox, expositors have attempted a systematic presentation to remedy this deficiency. But even some who profess a return to Pauline theology actually lose the biblical perspective when they derive social justice from love or benevolence. Brunner, more than most neo-orthodox spokesmen, has a Pauline doctrine of government, although *agape* comes to modify one or another of the applications of his theory also. But because of the prominence Brunner gives to both judgment and punishment, American liberal expositors of Christian social ethics are prone to criticize even Brunner's

8 P. Maury, *Politics and Evangelism* (New York: Doubleday, 1959), p. 61.

formulation as involving a "radical separation of love from justice."[9] Walter G. Muelder fails to understand the essentially preservative role of justice as contrasted with the restorative role of redemption, and hence he urges against Brunner that "except within the context of supportive love, judgment and punishment are [not] restorative of social order." E. Clinton Gardner criticizes Brunner for emphasizing the "restraining" character of justice rather than its "positive" role of the enrichment of human life.[10] But the complaint really rests not so much on Brunner's neglect of the dynamic importance of justice as upon Gardner's notion that social institutions generally, and the State especially, are obliged benevolently to meet the needs of individuals. The weakness in such theories, that urge a political order enabling citizens "to seek the fulfillment of their natures and purposes" under government welfare programs, lies in their failure to discern that to transcend justice in society is actually to substitute injustice — in the name of love or benevolence — for justice itself. Such is the accomplishment of legislation that maintains the interest of one section of the populace against those of another section. One is hardly surprised to find Gardner asserting that "all actual laws and systems of justice contain contradictions to *agape*,"[11] when he ought in fact to be conceding that the very restructuring he proposes both compromises justice and restricts the expression of love. We urgently need a comprehensive social ethics whose scriptural content protects justice from subtle compromises with benevolence.

In *The Biblical Doctrine of Justice and Law*, Schrey, Walz, and Whitehouse remind us: "Where love may forgive, justice calls for punishment. The tension between justice and love can be mitigated to a considerable degree by pointing out

[9] Walter G. Muelder, *Foundations of the Responsible Society* (New York: Abingdon Press, 1959), p. 97.
[10] E. C. Gardner, *Biblical Faith and Social Ethics* (New York: Harper & Bros., 1960), p. 260.
[11] *Ibid.*, p. 268.

how justice may be understood as the expression of love which is appropriate in circumstances where more is involved than simple personal relationship between two parties."[12] Concerning justice and love, they remark further: "These two norms of conduct seem in fact to have fallen apart. Though they may be held to coincide in the action of God, and though they are brought into coincidence once more in the human action of Jesus, that coincidence cannot be adequately expressed, as yet, in the common life of mankind. All that we can hope for is a close parallelism."[13]   But the writers then proceed to erase the distinction between justice and love by assigning to justice "a restorative element."   Much of the confusion in expositions of this kind arises from the treatment of the human race as a unit, and the consequent neglect of Augustine's important emphasis — in his contrast between the City of God and the Worldly City — that the human race is split in two.   Schrey, Walz, and Whitehouse comment: "But it is difficult to maintain the thesis that justice and love really coincide, in the circumstances of this sinful world, without falling into an absurd use of language in extreme cases; e.g., that the waging of a 'just' war, or the infliction of a just, though severe, punishment, are really acts of love."[14]   The authors create their own problem by expecting love and justice to be applied equally and universally — an objectionable premise that discredits retributive punishment by making it inconsistent with love and with the nature of God.   Surely, we would reply, a just war is an act of love to those who are defended.

In the United States, expositors of Christian social ethics often affirm the love-responsibility of the state without ex-

12 Heinze-Horst Schrey, Hans Hermann Walz, and W. A. Whitehouse, *The Biblical Doctrine of Justice and Law* (London: SCM Press, 1955), p. 182.
13 *Ibid.*, p. 182.
14 *Ibid.*

plaining why this responsibility exists and how it should be implemented. Walter G. Muelder urges "creative thought on how the state . . . can be constructively developed as a servant of justice and freedom, perhaps even of love."[15] Muelder himself contends that "the full personalistic norm of love is the final standard for justice in both moral and legal formulations."[16] Even the process of law, symbolized in the judge who represents the community, is expected "to fulfill the demands of love within the instruments of justice."[17]

John C. Bennett argues that "paternalistic expressions of Christian love" were once "the best way of improving the condition of the poor and oppressed. But today Christian love . . . cannot be content with philanthropy as a substitute for efforts to achieve more equal justice."[18] We must now think of God as working "through social necessities" to promote human welfare. Bennett's program of government love includes economic distribution with a view to greater equality of wealth.[19]

Social action agencies of the Protestant denominations often detail the implications of such theses, and an interlocking ecumenical personnel then frequently concurs in some platform of practical commitments. Unfortunately, these groups seldom expound the comprehensive theological positions from which such goals can be consistently drawn. And their pro-

---

[15] Muelder, *op. cit.*, p. 108.

[16] *Ibid.*, p. 92.

[17] *Ibid.*, p. 100.

[18] John C. Bennett, in A. Dudley Ward (ed.), *Goals of Economic Life* (New York: Harper & Bros., 1953), p. 410.

[19] *Ibid.*, pp. 421f. This writer recalls the initial meeting of the American Society of Christian Social Ethics, at which John C. Bennett urged redistribution of wealth. Thereupon I asked these questions: (1) Is it sinful or immoral for one person to have less than another? (2) Where is a just line to be drawn objectively in terms of an ideal "more" and "less"? (3) By what dynamism is such a balancing to be achieved? (4) What biblical instruction can be cited in support of the answers?

posals to fulfill the love-commandment through institutional structures, particularly political complexes, seem wholly to ignore the demonic potentials latent in organizational fulfillment.

Since the motif of the public good or of the public welfare appears both in religious and in political documents, it cannot be said to be exclusively sectarian or secular. In the Epistle to the Romans (13:4) the Apostle Paul says that the State's ministry is "for good," while in the preamble to the United States Constitution we read that government is to promote "the general welfare." But the Church has not historically understood the Pauline teaching to imply that Christian benevolences to the destitute and jobless are to be implemented ideally through a tax-supported program of government benefits. Nor have American political theorists in earlier generations been prone to stretch the phrase "public welfare" to cover "benevolent justice," as the widening program of government welfare benefits is sometimes described.

Not infrequently, ecclesiastical champions of state welfare complain that the viewpoint here presented betokens an insensitivity to Christian ethics in government and actually promotes a non-Christian state. But that is to miss the point. On occasion the State may even be "more Christian" than the churches themselves in political affairs. This happened, for example, when the United States government prevailed over the attempt made by some of the southern churches to preserve slavery. But in our time government would be "more Christian" if it had the political conscience to observe proper bounds between religious and governmental authority — that is, to insist firmly upon the distinction of justice and benevolence. Churchmen who speak of "christianizing" the political order today, regrettably, tend rather to approve the merging of justice and benevolence, and actually promote the socializing of the State. What needs to be discovered today is that nobody can "much improve" the State beyond the

158

point of *justice;* those who plead the gospel as a ground of their political views mistake both the nature of the State and the character of the gospel.

Since the rise of the "social gospel," Protestant ethical theory has lost vital contact with biblical perspectives. Instead, Protestant expositors have tended to promote the "practical idealism" of Anglo-Saxon social philosophy in the name of Christian religion. Christian social ethics, therefore, has preoccupied itself mainly with material betterment. Although now and then asserting a Christological foundation in broadest generalities, Protestant moralists have addressed the social situation in terms of particular programs having ecclesiastical approval rather than in terms of a theological interpretation of social order. Neither motivations nor goals are distinguished clearly in relation to justice or love. As a result, the content of Protestant social ethics has become scarcely distinguishable from the objectives of secular reform: development of retarded nations, conservation of natural resources, adequate housing, and higher wages are typical concerns. Political adjustment of economic differences is regarded as a proper expression of Christian love for neighbor, and even as a necessary aspect of "the kingdom of God." More recently, Barth's moderation of justice by love has supplied some social critics with a formal framework for promoting the extension of government benevolence, no longer on the ground of fixed moral principles but in terms of fluid middle axioms identified nonetheless with the will of God for our times.

Protestant social action agencies, therefore, have fallen prey to a curious inconsistency. While they promoted the extension of state welfare as a human right (that is, as a matter of justice), they also urged legislative implementation of public benevolence as a matter of Christian neighbor-love. No longer is it clear whether ecclesiastical leaders are engaging in social action for the common good as a specifically sectarian concern, or as an humanitarian obligation. Less doubtful, however, is the fact that they have derived the content of the "common good" from modern social theories rather than from biblical principles. On this theory the distinction between clearly defined human rights, human needs, and human wants soon vanishes. The totalitarian state blurs human "rights" and "welfare" into indistinguishable concepts, and makes both depend upon the sovereignty of the State. The consequences of such confusion in the political democracies can hardly be overstated. Totalitarian government recognizes no transcendently given human rights, and in the interest of the welfare state it destroys the benevolent ministry of voluntary agencies to persons in need. The citizen has no rights over against the State; the State alone decrees the citizen's welfare.

But if it is true that love must modify political and social justice, can human rights be preserved? Does not the State become increasingly responsible for the whole person? Does not this premise, if taken seriously, imply that a secular or sectarian religion may be imposed on the people (let alone totalitarian hostility toward religion)? Where a backslidden Christendom exists, the welfare state philosophy thus curiously gains secret momentum from the thesis that God is love. Most Protestant expositors of social ethics simply ignore the fact that when the government provides, less scope is given to personal compassion. While love as a government function would seem in theory to destroy the State's role of coercion, benevolence in state welfare actually becomes a handmaid of government compulsion rather than of freedom under God. The recent persecution of the Amish in Indiana is a noteworthy example. This development of compulsory benevolence is doubly remarkable in view of the fact that in the New Testament view the coercive role of the State is limited to its punitive function.

The Christian view involves the recognition, Cecil De Boer writes, that "that state is the best which permits the

160

greatest amount of freedom to the individual consonant with public order and sound morality. It holds that the continuity and progress of a society depend upon the individual rather than upon technics and organization. . . ." In a century when men seek the redemption of society through political structures, and give over to those structures the mission of ministering benevolently to their neighbors, it is refreshing to read De Boer's warning against the surrender of individual responsibility to the State: "A Christian society is a free society and a self-governing society just because it insists that as members of the body politic men are responsible for the well-being of their neighbors as potential sons of God endowed with a moral inviolability. And to refuse this accountability is to deny the divine demand of justice, a sin for which men and societies usually pay in the form of war, pestilence, and famine. A contemporary form of this sin is the popular yearning for the welfare state, *i.e.*, the habit of looking to the government for just about everything. Inasmuch as it amounts to a virtual deification of the state, the state may eventually become, as Luther reminds us, 'an instrument of punishment' to the people for the sin of refusing to govern themselves."[20] In the next generation the debilitating effect of the "welfare" state upon human character will be more readily apparent, and then the association of "cradle to crematory" social engineering with human welfare will come under deeper criticism. It would be sad indeed if in this emerging social criticism the churches were once again to yield the initiative to secular social reformers and should belatedly and sheepishly follow in their train.

4. PROPOSED RECONSTRUCTION OF THEOLOGY

Social theorists have also applied their emphasis on benevolence as a government function to capital punishment. Under

---

[20] C. DeBoer, *Responsible Protestantism* (Grand Rapids: Eerdmans, 1957), pp. 180f.

the vulnerable assumption that the object of punishment is to seek the good of the offender, Muelder argues that "except within the context of supportive love," judgment and punishment do not restore the person who has committed an offense[21] At the turn of the century Charles Hodge detected the relevant theological shift: while historically it was emphasized that offenders are penalized primarily to vindicate the righteousness of God, it became popular to assert that punishment exists for the good of society or the correction of the offender. The exposition in his *Systematic Theology* is even more timely now than it was then. Modern penal theories which stress a psychological or social evaluation of crime and dismiss the element of punishment were discussed critically in Stockholm in 1925 at the Universal Christian Conference on Life and Work. What would happen to the social order, we might ask, if sentimental revisionists some day reconstruct the science of penology to give criminals the benefit also of the Christian virtue of forgiveness (seventy times seven!) rather than insisting on the demand of justice for punishment.

It is noteworthy that whereas in the forepart of the century the liberal reconstruction of Protestant theology influenced the revision of social theory, it is *modern social perspectives* that *now often supply the encouragement for theological and doctrinal change*. L. Harold DeWolf notes, for example, that the dissatisfaction with the doctrines of final judgment and eternal punishment of the wicked has doubtless been influenced by "modern changes in ideals of penology.... Underneath these changes in penological and ethical thought is the growing influence of the Christian conviction that God is our loving Father."[22] And E. Clinton Gardner declares that "all existing systems of justice need to be transformed by love" and demands that the concept of justice acquire personal rather than

21 Muelder, *op. cit.*, p. 79.
22 L. Harold DeWolf, *A Theology of the Living Church* (New York: Harper and Brothers, 1953), pp. 280f.

impersonal application. He undergirds his plea for the trans-mutation of justice by noting the "wide agreement in modern penology that justice demands concern for the rehabilitation of the criminal rather than simple retribution."[23]

5. DILEMMAS IN SOCIAL ETHICS

To attach the claims of "love" or benevolence to the inter-pretation of justice in the sphere of government welfare activity has led to monstrous confusion. In East Germany, Protestants lament the fact that the Communist government, as a welfare state, arrogates all relief and welfare activity to government and deprives the churches of a ministry of benevo-lence. In America, on the other hand, many leaders of Prot-estant social service agencies flout opportunities for voluntarism through the special ministry of the churches, and rely in-creasingly upon partnership with government as a means of exercising Christian benevolence in society. The involve-ment and initiative of ecclesiastical agencies in this develop-ment have all but deprived American Protestantism of any consistent principle in social welfare activity.

The Great Depression of the 1930s in the United States demonstrated the inability of voluntary agencies to cope with a national emergency. While a wholly proper demand was created for special government aid to the needy and jobless during the period of economic crisis, the catastrophe also created an opportunity for social revisionists to promote theories of state welfare that involve the government in a continuing and perpetual role of dispensing benevolences. Whenever social welfare is permanently fixed as a dimension of state moral concern (and is not limited simply to emer-gencies with which voluntary agencies cannot cope), public pressures increase until government extends its provision to cover not only human rights and emergency needs, but even the wants of the many. The end result of such a process

[23] Gardner, *op. cit.*, p. 261.

is the welfare state. The role of government becomes widened beyond its scriptural responsibility for *social justice* to include a responsibility for *welfare* legislation.

This state-welfare activity, in turn, has been heralded by denominational spokesmen as an advance in the government's conception of social responsibility and as evidence that Christian motifs are permeating the State's outlook. These ecclesiastical state welfare enthusiasts have progressively involved their denominations in a program of "partnership" with government in fulfilling religious welfare burdens to such an extent that American Protestants espouse a welfare philosophy vastly different from their historic commitment, and much more agreeable to the Roman Catholic philosophy which traditionally disavows separation of Church and State.

The primary "justification" for this step, even if seldom articulated with precision, was that "Christianizing" the State's ministry is desirable, inasmuch as voluntary ministration can no longer cope with the large scope of human need. Obviously the churches would themselves be less and less disposed to respond to human need as a special duty if their own ecclesiastical leaders assure them not only that government will care for the needy, but also that State ministrations are indeed the Christian way of fulfilling religious benevolence responsibilities. But the fact is that such detachment of welfare activity from the churches permitted the champions of state welfare to broaden the understanding of welfare to dimensions exceeding its biblical scope and comprehension. Moreover, this government involvement indirectly enlisted the co-operation of the churches in implementing these wider objectives, without any apparent necessity of justifying this extension in terms of the Church's own historic understanding. But the fulfilling agency was now the State rather than the Church — even if the churches remained participating partners in certain phases of the program and ecclesiastical spokesmen conferred Christian approval and endorsement upon other aspects.

Between 1954 and 1959, as the federal government absorbed more and more functions once carried by private voluntary agencies, and as it expanded the scope of welfare laws to wider areas of coverage, the budget of the Department of Health, Education, and Welfare increased from $2 billion to almost $3½ billion. For fiscal 1963 the initial appropriation for the Department of $4,972,327,000, plus additional monies directed to it, brought the total budget to $5,107,811,000. The new feature in American life, therefore, is the merger of government and ecclesiastical leaders into a "social welfare" partnership; its controlling convictions are that through this development the State's ministrations assume the character of "benevolent justice," and that the Church, by promoting expanded government welfare services and by infusing spiritual content into these activities, unites "love and justice."

Because the churches cannot shoulder the vast welfare programs now carried by government, social action committees feel justified in accepting the expanding activity of state welfare. The possibility of establishing voluntary agencies (by churchgoers and non-churchgoers together) is seldom taken seriously except in isolated local situations. Nor does the conscience of church leadership ask if the supposed impracticality of voluntary effort is due to the State's extension and support of welfare far beyond human needs into the area of human wants. The Church's present disposition is to achieve her own welfare goals by means of tax-supported government programs. On one hand, the Church co-operates in widening the State's monopoly of welfare programs; on the other, the Church hopes to capture this government ministration for Christian propaganda purposes.[24] This co-operative arrange-

24 Since 1950, Lutheran World Relief has distributed more than $50 million worth of U. S. surplus foods. Its director recently told the Senate Foreign Relations Committee: "This pattern of partnership with government in a relief activity inevitably embodies some working relationships which may alter to some degree its character as a voluntary religious agency. . . . The voluntary agency may gradually, and per-

ment has meshed organized Protestantism into a program of welfare work with the State that involves new and astonishing Church-State relationships in America. Moreover, Protestant leaders now lack any consistent theory to articulate welfare responsibility. But the basic problem strikes deeper and arises from confusion over the concepts of justice and grace, of righteousness and love.

The Church's failure to differentiate clearly what she supports as justice in government welfare, from what she distinguishes as benevolence, is a costly mistake. It creates a twilight zone in which human rights and human desires are difficult to distinguish.

Has the Church any biblical basis for viewing *agape* as a government duty, or for making *apage* a citizen's rightful expectation from the State?

Is not the State's obligation in preserving justice to provide what is *due* (as corresponding to the *rights* of men) rather than to implement *agape* by acts of mercy or love?

Does not this ecclesiastical and secular confusion of justice and benevolence in defining the functions of government create a situation which weakens the Pauline premise, namely,

---

haps without being aware of it, tend to shift the burden of the support of its program from the gifts of its constituency to the contributions received from government, failing to recognize that its own witness is being gradually diluted thereby. Should it simultaneously fail to acknowledge and publicize at all times the source of the supplies which it distributes, it undermines its integrity from within, and its reputation from without. Since it is, above all, the purpose of a voluntary religious organization to give explicit testimony to the faith its members hold, it is virtually impossible for such an organization to prevent the impression abroad that its charitable activities result solely from its own inner life and resources. When it depends largely upon contributions from government to the operation of its program . . . this inevitably means the building up of the strength and reputation of religious organizations by the use of government contributions. We of Lutheran World Relief do not want this for ourselves and we cannot believe that any voluntary religious agency would wish such an outcome for itself" (*Christianity Today*, Vol. IV, No. 8, Jan. 18, 1960, p. 22).

that men are to support government in view of its divinely imposed duty to preserve justice? Does not this confusion reinforce instead, even if unwittingly, the Marxist premise that public welfare is a matter of state determination, and that government is the instrument of benevolence (that is, that government is to support the people)? Because the Church is obliged to communicate the gospel, it now seeks verbally to infuse spiritual content into secular welfare achievements. Can the Church in good conscience attach such a particularistic religious witness to state-supported welfare activities? Should the Church, moreover, seek to attach the preaching of the gospel to government supported welfare activity simply because a considerable share of public tax money comes from Christian believers? Should the Church attach a testimony of saving grace to what is one's due as a "right"? Would citizens who expect welfare benefits from the State as a "due" find in these provisions any tribute to mercy? In thus substituting state welfare activity for the responsibility of voluntary benevolence, has the Church really preserved its scriptural motivation of personal concern for neighbor that witnesses distinctively to God's unmerited provision of mercy in Christ?

The Church is in a dilemma. To make justice virtually akin to "righteous love" in the sphere of human action is a tenuous social strategy, in which justice soon loses its own status and in which the special interests of one class gradually replace those of another. Basic to this confusion is the sentimental modern reconstruction of the nature of God. This theological quagmire results from neo-orthodoxy's failure to rise above the modernist refusal to identify righteousness and justice no less than love with the essential core of God's being.

6. THE DECISIVE ISSUE

What distinguishes current statements of God's justice and love from those of recent past may be put this way. Classic liberal theology (1) denied any recognition of wrath whatever in divine experience; (2) merged divine righteousness into benevolence, so completely identifying God's nature with love that justice became simply one aspect of love's functions. But contemporary theology strikes deeper: (1) it reinstates wrath as a legitimate divine experience; (2) it differentiates justice from love (although sometimes only dialectically) so that righteousness no longer is wholly submerged in the divine will of love; (3) it even makes righteousness a constituent element of the nature of God. All this it affirms, however, within the prior assumption that (4) *love is fundamental to the divine nature*. Righteousness therefore becomes a constituent of the divine nature only as a constituent of love.[25] No doubt the newer statements advance beyond the sentimental speculations of Protestant liberalism concerning God's nature. But this theological readjustment still denies righteousness the same ultimacy as love in the nature of God. The subordination of divine righteousness to divine love leads to arbitrary conceptions of *agape* in which God's judgment and wrath do not come to full scriptural expression, and from which grossly unbiblical consequences are still deduced.

The continued denial that God is sovereign justice as well as sovereign love is one reason evangelical Protestants view the contemporary theological debate with anxiety. In the discussions of these attributes they desire not only to rediscover a biblical context and mood, but to reaffirm the biblical foundations as well. In an age skeptical of all inherited concepts of law and order, and which wavers between the choice of majority opinion or cynical anarchy, the Church needs nothing less than the authority of the Bible to speak about universally valid standards of justice. True,

---

25 It is true that the Old Testament moderates Israel's attitude of justice by the requirement of lovingkindness (to "the stranger in the land"). But this is an obligation imposed on the covenant community as a reflex of divine grace.

the biblical data is neither simple nor systematic, and theological decisions ventured on this basis are often exposed to vexing new situations in modern life. But the Bible unmistakably states the spiritual foundation of the world order. Justice belongs to the very being of God, whose righteousness is the sure source of law. He commands justice among his creatures; he will judge human justice eschatologically by divine justice. The Bible, moreover, discredits any theological maneuver that would demote either the righteousness or the love of God to inferior status by viewing divine love either as a matter of necessity or of caprice, or divine righteousness as a mere differentiation of love. Scripture warns against so fusing and confusing righteousness and love that the dominance of either nullifies the other. The Bible stands sentry against speaking of God's love as the foremost or conditioning divine attribute; it discredits fitting God's justice to love's convenience. Whenever love triumphs at the expense of holiness, whenever love takes priority over righteousness, we have moved outside the scriptural orbit.

So far we have merely called attention to the errors of those who sacrifice justice to love, and have analyzed some of the ultimate results of the current confusion over justice and love. To misstate the biblical view of the equal status of righteousness and love in God's being brings only continuing problems in dogmatics. Redemption soon loses its voluntary character as divine election and becomes an inevitable if not necessary divine provision. Discussion of Christ's death and atonement in modernism is uncomfortable in the presence of such themes as satisfaction and propitiation. Future punishment of the wicked is revised to conform to benevolent rather than punitive motivations, and hell is emptied of its terrors by man-made theories of universal salvation. The State is no longer dedicated to justice and order, encouraging and enforcing human rights and responsibilities under God, but is benevolently bent toward people's socio-economic wants.

It should be apparent enough, then, why evangelical theology stresses righteousness and love as equally ultimate in the being of God and wholly identical with his nature. Every divine act is an act of the Living God, who is the acme both of righteousness and love.

God's justice is the self-consistency of his acts: he addresses his moral law to all moral creatures, and holds all equally accountable — without special favor, personal preference, or partisanship. This is the very essence of justice, on which rests the whole concept of law and social order. All men are equally obligated; under these circumstances one man is entitled to the very same verdict as any other man irrespective of time and place. Human rights are universal; man's due, therefore, is his *due* as a universal due. One man's duties are the duties of his neighbor also, and of all men. These concepts are intrinsic to justice and law. To weaken any of them in principle is to weaken the foundations of an orderly society.

God's grace, on the other hand, is elective. Its great distinction is that it is addressed to some rather than to all, to a part rather than to the whole — not because they have some antecedent claim or right to this benefit but despite the fact that they do not.

The noted church historian Philip Schaff wrote that "the family, the church, and the state are divine institutions demanding alike our obedience, in their proper sphere of jurisdiction. . . . The church is the reign of love; the state is the reign of justice. The former is governed by the gospel, the latter by the law. . . . Both meet on questions of public morals, and both together constitute civilized human society and ensure its prosperity. . . . The root of this theory we find in the New Testament."[26]

The plain fact is that in the social order all prattling

26 Philip Schaff, *Church and State in the United States* (New York and London: G. P. Putnam's Sons. 1888) , p. 10; contained in *American Historical Association Papers* (same publisher) , Vol. II, No. 4, p. 392.

about love is irrelevant when what is needed is justice. The withholding of justice may be an expression of lovelessness, and the performance of justice may be described as love in action. But justice is not on that account formally identical with love, or vice versa. Nor are they identical in content: love goes beyond justice, although it does not negate it. Sinful men cannot really grasp the true nature of love, therefore, unless they are first taught the responsibility of justice through their common subjection to impartial laws that deal with all human beings alike; indeed, the transmutation of justice can only lead as well to the perversion of love. Justice deals with one's neighbor as a member of society as a whole, whereas love deals with him as a particular person.

Let it be said in summary, then, that theology that obscures the distinction between justice and grace soon sponsors alien views of social ethics, and any social theory that confounds justice and benevolence will work against a true understanding both of the nature of God and of the character of the gospel.

APPENDIX: CHRISTIANITY
AND REVOLUTION

THE QUESTIONS OF THE FORCIBLE DISPLACEMENT OF TYRANTS and of revolution against unjust governments have repeatedly arisen in Christian conscience and experience.[1] As a rule, Christianity has not advocated either revolution against the State or forcibly conforming the existing social order to divine law, but has recognized secular government as lawful and legitimate, provided its power is not perverted. The English Peasants' War, the German Peasants' Revolt, and seventeenth century Puritanism, which promoted the overthrow of secular government and the political substitution of a "divine social order," were exceptions to the rule. It is well known that Luther condemned Anabaptist preaching of "revolution in the name of Christ," whose objective was the forced imposition of a Christian order upon society in general.

1. ON TOPPLING TYRANTS AND TYRANNICAL GOVERNMENTS

The larger question of the Christian's attitude toward perverted government has been forced upon the Church almost continually by political developments in one land or another. Meinhold offers an illuminating study of the propriety or impropriety of "a Christian revolution" that "demands the

[1] Peter Meinhold rightly distinguishes this problem from the particular attempts of some religious visionaries to force the rule of Christ upon society in the form of a political theocracy in *Caesar's or God's?* (Minneapolis: Augsburg Press, 1962).

172

forcible removal of the tyrant or of a tyrannical system of government."[2]   He recalls Erich Kordt's disclosures, in his book *Not From Files,* of the debate among German leaders over whether they were obliged to destroy Hitler for refusing to listen to their arguments and launching a major offensive war.   Meinhold summarizes the teaching of the medieval theologians, particularly Thomas Aquinas, and distinguishes their teaching from John Parvus's later elevation of political murder to justifiable tyrannicide.   Under specific conditions Thomas Aquinas apparently condones a tyrant's forced removal and even his destruction.   The papal encyclicals, Meinhold notes, are not explicit about the limits and nature of active Christian resistance to unjust rulers and totalitarian governments.   He argues, moreover, that the exposition of the Catholic view by the moral theologian Rupert Augermair needs further clarification.   Meinhold pointedly asks: What constitutes a government's "perversion of power"?   What yardstick determines the common welfare?   Specifically, whose right is it to eliminate a perverse government?   Does "elimination" mean destroying only the rulers or the whole totalitarian system?[3]

Totalitarian developments in Europe have forced a searching and sharpening of the teaching of the Protestant Reformers about the limits of governmental power and of Christian obedience.   Luther's rejection of Christian attempts to revolutionize the social and political order did not imply, as some have contended, indifference to tyrannicide, for he advocated resistance against a ruler who imposes spiritual tyranny.[4]   The Reformed view, as expounded by Zwingli and Calvin, noted (as did Luther) the right of Christians to resist a tyrannical government, although Calvin more clearly defined the ruler's perversion in terms of opposition to the

2 *Ibid.,* p. 92.
3 *Ibid.,* p. 103.
4 *Ibid.,* pp. 108f.

tables of the law; Beza, moreover, assigned all Christians the duty of opposing tyrannical rulers.

The rise of the Nazis posed the issue in concrete historical form. During World War II, after the Nazis had imposed their rule upon the Norwegians, Bishop Berggrav called clergy and laity to resist the "false governing authorities." In the face of Nazi pretensions, Karl Barth appealed to the *Scottish Confession* of 1560. Article XIV lists the suppression of tyrants among the good works implicit in the second table of the law, and in this Barth saw a demand for active Christian resistance to modern tyrannical powers, and for non-recognition (as legitimate) of governing authorities that violate God's law. Under certain conditions Barth concedes the propriety of forcibly ending a perverse government: if this perversion is so pervasive that it practically eliminates individual freedom; if God categorically commands the revolution as a matter of divine obedience; and if the whole tyrannical political system is destroyed.

The subsequent rise of Communism has set in even sharper focus the question of the Christian's right and duty to resist perverse governing powers. Meinhold notes that Barth's third condition poses "an almost impossible and most difficult task" in view of the power accumulated by the modern totalitarian state.[5] He calls, therefore, for a more explicit definition of perversion of power, and asks whether the totalitarian state may not be unacceptable as such, and perverse simply because it unites all power in a single person or governmental system.[6] And, while granting to Barth that whoever revolts against a totalitarian ruler or system must do so in responsibility to God and man alone, he nonetheless finds Barth obscure in his stipulation of the source of an individual's authority to eliminate a tyrant. May not Barth's appeal to "the subjective hearing of the Word of God . . .

5 *Ibid.*, p. 116.
6 *Ibid.*, p. 117.

imply the danger of fostering a new political and religious enthusiasm, a *Schwaermertum*, over which the Church has no control and which . . . may abuse the Bible for its own ends?"[7]

Meinhold stipulates some of the critical issues remaining to be resolved in respect to the extermination of once legal but now illegitimate governments: Is there a Christian "right" to eliminate the tyrant? If so, does this not also imply a duty? For an individual, or for everyone? In what way is this duty to be discharged? By those in important positions, skilled in questions of law and rights and freedom? Meinhold specially emphasizes that all resistance based on religious and political considerations has "tremendous symbolic power" even if it does not lead to overthrow or removal of tyranny, since it illuminates what is right and wrong. He adds: "Every fight against a tyrant and a totalitarian system does not merely constitute a protest against perversion of law and suppression of freedom, but is also an appeal . . . to the conscience of all people not to surrender their rights and freedoms but to insist that these be respected by the government. Perhaps especially in the modern totalitarian state a special meaning is given to this symbolic power of resistance. For the sake of this symbolic power it must be carried out under all circumstances."[8]

2. IS CHRISTIANITY A REVOLUTIONARY RELIGION?

The Christian gospel is often described today as revolutionary. This term has been used to designate the radical conflict between Christianity and man's ideas of religion, human nature and culture. It is doubtless true, because the social agonies of our age run so deep, that no prospect of healing exists unless some redemptive force penetrates and pervades the arenas of modern life in equal or greater depth. But it

[7] *Ibid.*, pp. 117f.
[8] *Ibid.*, pp. 119, 120.

is misleading in the present context of world events to contend, as some do, that Christianity promotes genuine revolution, while socio-political upheavals at most are pseudo-revolutionary. To speak of Christian impact as a "deeper" revolution, or as "genuine" revolution, is in fact dangerous. This way of describing the situation admittedly retains in principle a proper emphasis on the radical character of the Christian demand for a twice-born race of men. But it does not really come to grips with the Christian attitude toward the spirit of revolution rampant today. Moreover, it may encourage a misunderstanding of the Christian message in terms of mere political theory, and thereby also misrepresent the Christian Church's attitude toward secular government.

Does the Christian religion really advocate political revolution, that is, the violent substitution of one government for another? While under some conditions Christian conscience may indeed approve certain *consequences* of revolution, Christian social theory neither promotes nor approves revolution itself as a method of social transformation. In Old Testament times the theocratic Hebrew nation, in the face of unbridled Gentile iniquity and barbarism, periodically considered itself under divine mandate to overthrow offensive pagan rulers and to destroy their ungodly people. But it does not follow therefrom that revolution as such is a biblically-approved strategy of social change. The Christian revelation never identifies true religion theocratically with any single nation. Moreover, it associates the revolutionary overthrow of national wickedness only with the vision of the returning Messiah, whose second advent in power and glory will mark the judgment of all nations.

At times certain leaders have indeed given their full blessing to certain revolutions. One thinks, for example, of the Greek revolution of 1821 which liberated Greece from Turkish domination, or of the American Revolution of 1776 which freed the colonies from arbitrary British rule. In the period immediately preceding the American Revolution the clergy not only emphasized the overall relevance of Christian doctrine to political order but also insisted on man's primary allegiance to divine authority and on the limits of governmental authority.[9]

It was mainly through early American religious thought, Felix Morley tells us, that limitation of civil power and authority became a central characteristic of the American way of life.[10] Said Jonathan Mayhew in the West Church of Boston on January 30, 1750, the anniversary of the execution of King Charles I: "Those in authority may abuse their trust and power to such a degree that neither the law of reason nor of religion requires that any obedience or submission be paid to them; but on the contrary that they should be totally discarded, and the authority which they were before vested with transferred to others, who may exercise more to those good purposes for which it is given." This sermon was printed and widely distributed under the title, "A Discourse Concerning Unlimited Submission." The dangers of unlimited official power and the moral limits of political submission were frequent pulpit themes during this pre-Revolutionary period.[11]

[9] Cf. Franklin P. Cole, *They Preached Liberty* (New York: Fleming H. Revell, 1941).

[10] F. Morley, *The Power in the People* (New York: Van Nostrand, 1949), pp. 136ff.

[11] John Wesley's attitude toward the American Revolution is illuminating. Wesley's guiding principle was that the people had a right to seek the redress of injustice, but not the right of revolution. While he sympathized with the colonists in their complaints of unjust treatment and deprivation of legal rights, nonetheless, after the war of 1776 and the signing of the Declaration of Independence, he opposed the new American government. It was based on a false notion of freedom, he said, that sought privileges (exemption from parliamentary taxation) which he now considered to be illegal and illicit. It is noteworthy that Wesley's efforts to revive Christian dedication and the sense of morality and calling are widely credited with having saved England from revolution such as swept over France.

Since government's function is to preserve order as well as to promote justice, Christian social theory opposes social change by anarchic methods. When revolution is regarded as a self-sufficient objective (and hence is represented as itself a panacea for social evil) it becomes insupportable and intolerable. Moreover, when revolution is detached from spiritual and moral obligations and proffers exemption from social responsibility it breeds irresponsibility and bestiality and must therefore invite Christian condemnation.[12] Christianity's interest in social change always carries with it the demand for inner renewal, and not simply external readjustments. But contemporary revolutions, advancing anti-Christian concepts of life and society, seem usually to promote social disorder and to displace one form of political injustice by another. The French Revolution, for example, represented not so much an overthrow of pervasive evils as a culmination of corrupt trends; as a social upheaval it revealed and augmented no genuine change in the underlying temper of spiritual and moral revolt. The inevitable clash between Christian social theory and Communist revolutionary premises is therefore immediately apparent. Christianity must repudiate any social upheaval whose motivation stems from state absolutism rather than the moral basis of law, and whose distinctions between good and evil, between justice and injustice are determined by an all-sovereign state.

Nonetheless, Christian social theory is free to approve certain results of revolution, including the abolition of tyranny. Social resentment thrives wherever and whenever citizens are deprived of elemental human rights. Totalitarian demands for behavior that violates biblical imperatives arouse indignation and resistance. Such resistance in turn may contribute to a

12 Cf. *Toward a Christian Civilization,* A Draft issued by the Christian Union of Professional Men of Greece (Athens: 'Damascus' Publications, 1950) , pp. 94f.

counter-revolution that tries to restore authority to the side of law and justice. The objective of such Christian action is not merely to overthrow one revolutionary form of government in favor of another, but rather to restore government to its proper concerns. By fostering a spirit which makes a totalitarian outcome impossible, Christianity may indirectly contribute to revolution in a totalitarian climate by creating respect for law (cf. Jer. 22). The fact that the Christian religion inherently recognizes a moral will superior to the will of the State largely explains the antipathy of some modern revolutionaries toward Christianity. W. R. Inge noted long ago that Marxist leaders "see very clearly that Christianity takes all the sting and fury out of revolutionary agitation."[13]

Revolution can hope for Christian sympathy only where it actually protests against an established government's persistent abuse of the norms of government (maintenance of law and order, protection of the innocent, repression of bad works) and where it openly purposes to re-establish these norms. At its worst, as Berdyaev reminds us, the State may become almost a demonic power whose organization gives new and terrible strength to the world's hostility to God. But as O. C. Quick observes, the fallen state, like fallen man, "is never simply evil, even when its government may be said to have forfeited its moral claim on the obedience of its citizens. Every form either of rebellion or of passive resistance to the government must justify itself as a protest made in the name of the State as it might and ought to be — it seeks the reorganization of the State itself on a juster model."[14] Although evangelical social conscience will not initiate revolution, the Christian community will support legitimate demands for social justice based on transcendent divine law.

---

[13] W. R. Inge, *The Church and the Age* (London: Longmans, Green, 1912), p. 75.
[14] O. C. Quick, *Christianity and Justice* (London: Sheldon Press, 1940), p. 62.

3. SOME NEW TESTAMENT PERSPECTIVES

During the three hundred years when the Roman emperors declared Christianity an illegal religion, Christians were marked as criminals by civil law simply because they were Christians. Against such government the Christian movement generated no revolutionary temper, and to such government Christian believers pledged their prayers and paid their taxes.[15] The Christian does not promote the cause of anarchy, since he knows that government has a biblical role. Even if a government now and then exceeds its proper authority, the Christian's hope of a better tomorrow is sustained by a firm reliance on divine providence more than by enthusiasm for human revolution. The Book of Revelation (ch. 13) depicts the saints as preparing for martyrdom rather than for revolution when the Antichrist confronts them.

While Jesus did not regard the State "as in any sense a final, divine institution," he nonetheless, as Oscar Cullmann emphasizes, "accepts the state and radically renounces every attempt to overthrow it . . . . This double attitude is characteristic of the entire New Testament."[16] Jesus' Palm Sunday entrance into Jerusalem "on a donkey and not as a warlike Messiah on a horse — as he is described in Zechariah 9:9 — could speak

[15] It is noteworthy that Jesus' words, "render unto Caesar" (Matt. 22:17), came during the reign of Tiberius Caesar (A.D. 14-37). It was during this Caesar's rule, Tacitus notes, that the inhabitants of Syria and Judea petitioned Rome for reduction of excessive taxes (*Annals*, ii. 42) which, according to F. C. Grant, ran 30 or 40 per cent of income, and perhaps even higher (*The Economic Background of the Gospels*, London, Oxford University Press, 1926, p. 105). Bruce M. Metzger writes: "There was a tax or duty upon all imports and exports; on all that was grown on the soil, . . . a poll tax levied on all persons (bond and free), and . . . a tax on personal property. . . . A house duty was paid by the inhabitants . . . [and] taxes on axles, wheels, pack-animals, pedestrians, roads, highways; admission to markets; on carriers, bridges, ships, and quays; on crossing rivers, on dams, on licenses . . . ." ("The Christian and Society," a paper read to the Lake Forest Consultation in 1962).

[16] O. Cullmann, *The State in the New Testament* (New York: Chas. Scribner's Sons, 1956), pp. 18f.

against a revolutionary intention."[17]   It is the more remarkable, therefore, that on the basis of representations by the Jewish Sanhedrin the Roman authorities apparently crucified Jesus as a zealot, that is, as one seeking by holy war to overthrow the Roman Empire in order to establish an earthly Kingdom of Heaven.[18]

That Jesus "suffered under Pontius Pilate" holds a political warning for his disciples also; they must constantly reckon with the possibility of persecution by the State (Matt. 10:18). Yet the Christian need not always "suffer injustice." Obedience and silence are not forever the only course open to him in the face of unlawfully constituted authority.   Under some circumstances, in fact, disobedience to government becomes a Christian duty.   In Cullmann's words: "It is not our business to take the sword, to wage war as the fellowship of Christians against this [totalitarian] State in order to destroy its existence." Our obligation, rather, is "positively, perseverance in our Christian preaching; negatively, perseverance in our refusal of the idolatry demanded by the State."[19]   The Acts of the Apostles leaves no doubt that rulers are to be disobeyed when they forbid the proclamation of the gospel.   Christians then resist the ruler not in opposition to civil law but in obedience to God's command.   "As soon as the State demands more than is necessary to its existence," observes Cullmann, "as soon as it demands what is God's — thus transgressing its limits — the disciple of Jesus is relieved of all obligation to this requirement of a totalitarian State."[20]   Cullmann contrasts the crucifixion of Jesus — on the false ground that he was a zealot — with the later martyrdom of Christians who resisted the Roman emperors' totalitarian demand for worship of Caesar.   He contends that "collaborationist" theological ad-

[17] *Ibid.,* p. 38.
[18] *Ibid.,* pp. 12, 43.
[19] *Ibid.,* p. 84.
[20] *Ibid.,* p. 51.

visers to totalitarian rulers "have no ground for appealing to Romans 13" to secure Christian endorsement and participation in the crimes of a totalitarian State.[21]

The Christian approach to government differs from the anarchist concept in several ways. It gladly obeys where government observes its proper limits, protests where it exceeds those limits, and actively resists where a totalitarian demand requires disobedience to the revealed will of God. "In the Roman State emperor worship is the point at which the State exceeds its proper bounds. . . . For the rest, the Roman State was a legitimate State, knowing how to distinguish between good and evil."[22] The German national-socialistic state, however, legally fell away "from the order in which every State is placed; for here the distinction between good and evil, right and wrong, no longer prevailed: on the contrary, right was whatever the State required."[23] The Bible, it is noteworthy, treats totalitarian powers not simply as extreme forms of human pretension, nor only in relation to the Antichrist, but as the intrusion of Satan himself into the realm of government. In both the Jewish and early Christian view, Cullmann remarks, the totalitarian State is precisely "the classic form of the Devil's manifestation on earth."[24] "Where others see that a state is becoming 'totalitarian' the Christian sees that the powers, subjected by Christ to God's service, are once again breaking loose and becoming satanic."[25]

4. PRESSURES IN THE MODERN WORLD

Today in many lands the pressures of totalitarian government weigh almost intolerably upon the consciences of many Christians. "Not since the Church was persecuted by the

21 *Ibid.*, p. 56.
22 *Ibid.*, p. 78.
23 *Ibid.*
24 *Ibid.*, p. 74.
25 *Ibid.*, p. 90.

Roman Empire have the forces in culture seeking to destroy the distinctive moral witness of Christians been so strong as they are in this generation."[26] There is every prospect that in the near future Christians in many places will find themselves more and more in politically intolerable situations. Some Christian leaders even suggest the coming of a new Babylonian captivity for the Church. In Angola, more than sixty-seven pastors were imprisoned and at least forty were killed; for fifteen months there was absolutely no sign of seventy of these Christian leaders. In several countries, despite the jeopardy to their husbands, missionary wives have pleaded with their mission boards to address government leaders directly concerning the perils that face the whole Christian community. Sensing the rise of totalitarian regimes, some mission leaders are asking if they ought to lead their people in revolt. In Cuba, Castro has tried to silence Protestant missionaries because he considers them counter-revolutionary.

In times like these the Church must define its position before the world, and, moreover, in terms of the gospel and its implications. But several problems arise when the corporate Church claims emergency "justification" for speaking to government officialdom. For one thing, who determines what shall be said? We are reminded of Jesus, who told his disciples, "You will be brought before governors and kings, for my sake, to testify before them and the heathen. But when you are arrested, do not worry about what you are to say; when the time comes, the words you need will be given you; for it is not you who will be speaking: it will be the Spirit of your Father speaking in you" (Matt. 10:18ff., NEB). In Jesus' day Christians turned from the Jewish Sanhedrin which condemned Christ to death. And Protestants have never had a Pope. Who is authorized to speak authoritatively and infallibly for the Holy Spirit in ecclesiastical circles? Who is

---

[26] Edward LeRoy Long, Jr., *Conscience and Compromise* (Philadelphia: Westminster Press, 1954), p. 7.

to articulate what the corporate Church must communicate to the rulers of nations? A second problem is this: who determines under what emergencies or situations the corporate Church may address political bodies directly? Some single out as a justifiable occasion the serious degradation of law in Germany in the 1930s. Others point to South Africa's complete separation of the races with its attendant disruption of homes and culture. Others speak in terms of any illegal act that infringes upon civil rights, and on that basis justify the Church's encouragement of "sit-in" demonstrations, for example. It is one thing for ecclesiastical leaders to confront twentieth century governments at the apostolic level, that is, to declare that the Church if hindered from preaching the gospel will disobey government even to the point of martyrdom in order to obey God. It is quite another matter when the corporate Church and government leaders pitch their communication at another level.

Karl Barth has said that Christians should co-operate even with a Communist government so long as it allows the preaching of the gospel. There is always the danger, however, that while it is allowing Christians to carry on their activities unimpeded for a season, a state may march unchallenged toward its implementation of totalitarianism. In Germany even evangelical Christians thought Hitler was good for the nation. He promised them liberty, and moreover, opposed Communism with its objective to expropriate private property. Evangelical chaplains accordingly served loyally with others in Hitler's army, while Barth and some neo-orthodox leaders protested the totalitarian development in the name of divine revelation. In Japan, on the other hand, it was the liberals who supported the government while evangelicals opposed its religious pretensions and totalitarian features.

Philippe Maury emphasizes that the Christian owes the State limited, not absolute, obedience: "When political events threaten the essence of the gospel, when the State promulgates laws which undermine the very foundations of Christian faith and pervert the nature of the church, as was the case with Hitler's anti-Semitic regulations, the church has no other course but to protest officially and to reaffirm, in face of political paganism, the fulness of the gospel, even going so far as to call its members to disobey the state. A church which fails to do so ceases to be the Church of Christ."[27]

Yet the Christian does not then face totalitarian forces in the human spirit of counter-revolution. The New Testament does not approve renouncing the State as an institution, and limits the resistance shown even to a totalitarian state. And even when he needs to resist totalitarian demands, the Christian must always pray for the State. The united purposive prayer of a minority Christian community within a totalitarian climate may be as far-reaching and powerful as the political tyrants who shape the course of their totalitarian states. In praying for the conversion of pagan rulers, moreover, the Christian need not expect, as did the Roman Church in medieval times, that the ruler's religion automatically become that of the people. In advocating irreligion, Communist officials have given this vulnerable medieval theory a rather unforeseen application. Only Christ at his coming has the authority to put an end to civil government, to assess earthly rulers in final judgment, and to consign any nation forever to his "left side." The fact that a totalitarian regime (even when it insincerely professes to be a "people's democratic republic") confronts its citizens everywhere with the all-embracing power of the State need not wholly limit the Christian in his personal witness to the gospel nor deprive him of political significance. The believer's lack of opportunity for the kind of effective political action which is granted to all citizens in truly democratic lands need not deprive him entirely of political perspective. "For he knows," as Jan D. Dengerink has remarked,

---

[27] P. Maury, *Politics and Evangelism* (Garden City, N. Y.: Doubleday, 1959) , p. 69.

"that even totalitarian forces are wholly enclosed within God's omnipotence. And he can become a witness of that divine sovereignty as long as God grants him life, even in the face of totalitarian governments, as Christ remained such a witness also when he, forsaken by all, stood before Pontius Pilate (John 19:11)."[28]

Although not committed to revolution in principle, the Christian need not therefore pledge his heart more than one day at a time to a regime whose attitudes toward the Church may be dictated simply by temporary strategy and whose eventual and permanent intentions are not clear.

The Christian Church is not anarchistic. The Christian Church is not revolutionary. The Christian Church does not initiate movements for political independence. "My kingdom does not belong to this world," said Jesus (John 18:36, NEB). Yet Christianity is not ashamed or apologetic, as if on that account it merely laps up the privileges that others have earned. For the Church remains ready to proclaim and ready to be martyred for proclaiming those abiding truths and ultimate loyalties whose surrender reduces every revolution to lawlessness and whose loss casts even a free people into subjection and nihilism.

28 J. D. Dengerink, "The Power of the Reformation in Political Life," in *International Reformed Bulletin*, V (April, 1962), 7.

INDEX OF NAMES

INDEX OF SUBJECTS

23296